CREATION
**Nature's Designs
and Designer**

Editor and Designer:	Richard H. Utt
Chief Science Consultant:	Richard M. Ritland
Writers:	Robert E. D. Clark Harold G. Coffin L. E. Downs Leonard N. Hare Eric A. Magnusson Richard M. Ritland Joan Beltz Roberts Asa C. Thoresen James R. Van Hise T. Joe Willey
Copy Editors:	Milton Gilstrap Kenneth Wilson
Art Director and Illustrator:	Howard Larkin

CREATION

Nature's Designs and Designer

**PACIFIC PRESS
PUBLISHING ASSOCIATION**
Mountain View, California
Omaha, Nebraska
Oshawa, Ontario

Copyright © 1971 by

PACIFIC PRESS
PUBLISHING ASSOCIATION

Litho in
United States of America

All Rights Reserved

Library of Congress
Catalog Card No. 70-136566

Contents

1. Designed for Flight 8
2. Inside a "Simple" Cell 25
3. Photosynthesis—Bread From Light 38
4. The Heart of the Problem 48
5. Fossils From the Ancient Seas 59
6. Proteins and Probability 67
7. What "Natural Selection" Cannot Do 81
8. Fail-safe and Foolproof 87
9. Modern Science: An Enlarging Vista 97
10. Those Missing Links 107
11. Dimensions of the Mind 116

    Contributors 134

    Credits 136

    Index 137

Preface

by Dr. Wernher von Braun
National Aeronautics and Space Administration
Washington, D.C.

Manned space flight is an amazing achievement, but it has opened for mankind thus far only a tiny door for viewing the awesome reaches of space. An outlook through this peephole at the vast mysteries of the universe should only confirm our belief in the certainty of its Creator.

I find it as difficult to understand a scientist who does not acknowledge the presence of a superior rationality behind the existence of the universe as it is to comprehend a theologian who would deny the advances of science. And there is certainly no scientific reason why God cannot retain the same relevance in our modern world that He held before we began probing His creation with telescope, cyclotron, and space vehicles.

Our survival here and hereafter depends on adherence to ethical and spiritual values. Through science man tries to harness the forces of nature around him; through religion he tries to control the forces of nature within him and find the moral strength and spiritual guidance for the task that God has given him.

1. Designed for Flight

Asa C. Thoresen

According to an ancient Greek myth, Daedalus, an architect and sculptor of Athens, fell out of favor with Minos, king of Crete. He and his son Icarus were imprisoned in a maze called the Labyrinth, but they determined to be free. Daedalus closely studied the wings of sea birds and, with wax and feathers, made two pairs of wings of similar design. Flapping these wings, father and son soared into the air, intending to escape to the island of Sicily.

Then came disaster. Icarus, excited with his ability to fly, forgot his father's warning and flew too near the sun. The result, according to the poet, was that "with melting wax and loosened strings, sank hapless Icarus on unfaithful wings."

Grieving Daedalus landed safely in Sicily, but Icarus drowned in the Mediterranean.

This old myth illustrates the longing earthbound human beings have always felt to soar into the sky like the birds. Over 2,000 years after the days of Minos and the legendary Daedalus, man *did* learn how to fly, but not by attaching wings to his shoulders. Eventually human beings faced the fact that, besides having no wings, their bodies are in no way designed for flight. For example, the breast muscles which operate the shoulders and arms in man constitute less than one percent of his body weight, while those of some birds weigh as much as thirty-three percent!

CREATION—NATURE'S DESIGNS AND DESIGNER

From the tip of their beaks to the end of their tail feathers, birds show remarkable aerodynamic design. Birds (except for a few kinds like the ostrich that do not fly) are equipped with intricately constructed feathers; powerful wings; light, hollow bones; rigid skeletal parts; large, strong hearts for circulation of warm blood; a remarkable respiratory system; and a digestive system that quickly absorbs the energy from food.

The man-o'-war bird's seven-foot wings weigh a few ounces.

Although the man-o'-war bird has a wingspan of up to seven feet, its bones weigh only four or five ounces. "Light as a feather," we say. But this bird's skeleton actually weighs less than its feathers! In addition, the bones are flexible and very strong; they must be able to cope with the stresses and strains of maneuverable flight. A bird's skull weighs about one sixth as much as the skull of a mammal of comparable size. The tail vertebrae and pelvic bones are joined into an extremely light cylindrical structure. The breastbone anchors the powerful wing muscles and extends backward, giving support to the internal organs while in horizontal flight. The long bones of the legs and wings are hollow, each one supported within by trusses and struts for extra strength.

Penetrating the hollow bones, even the small toe bones, is a remarkable system of air sacs which are actually extensions of the respiratory system. These give buoyancy both in air and water and increase the respiratory and cooling surface area. This system helps the exchange of oxygen and carbon dioxide from the body tissues. Only one quarter of the air intake is used for breathing. The remaining three quarters serves to cool the active tissues.

Birds' high temperature and rapid circulation make them far more efficient than any airplane.

To cope with the tremendous energy demanded for flight, birds have the highest body temperatures of any creature. A man's normal temperature is 98-99° Fahrenheit, but a bird's may rise to 110°. This temperature, along with a good digestive system and rapid circulation, enables birds to utilize an unusually high percentage of the energy in their food. Water birds digest even the bones of the fish they eat. Concentrated urine passes directly from the kidneys to the exterior, without passing through a bladder. This also saves weight.

The golden plover migrates thousands of miles across the ocean from Labrador to the central part of South America, losing only *two ounces* of its body weight in the process! If a small airplane were as efficient as the plover, it would fly 160 miles on one gallon of gasoline.

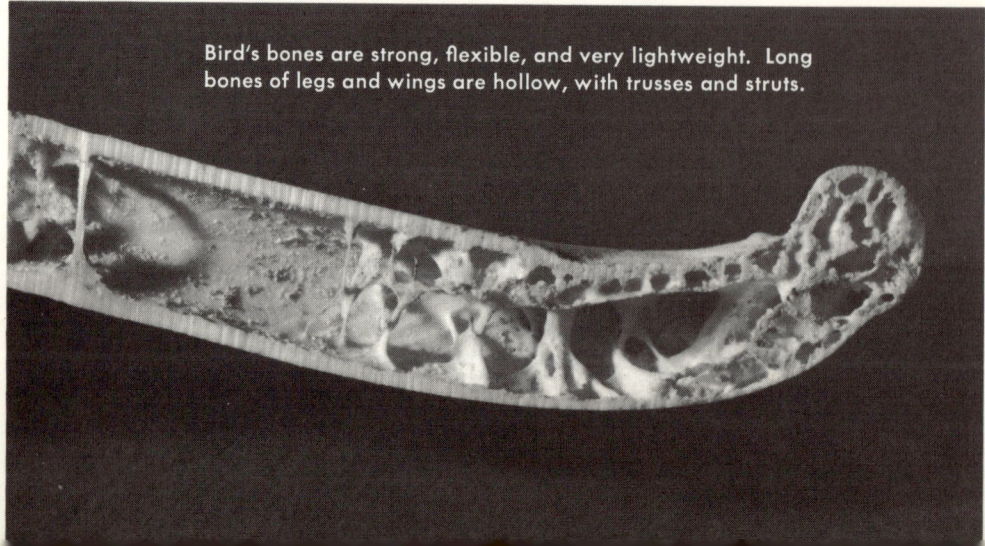

Bird's bones are strong, flexible, and very lightweight. Long bones of legs and wings are hollow, with trusses and struts.

Strong breast muscles, used in flying and soaring, account for up to a third of the body weight of birds.

In some birds, up to one third of the body weight is made up of the breast muscles which operate the wings. The largest of these muscles is called the pectoralis major. Some birds, such as the shearwaters, have smaller breast muscles and strong tendons to keep the wings extended for long periods of time. They soar on thermal currents like gliders or sailplanes.

Birds have a higher blood pressure than man's, and blood sugar concentrations twice that of average mammals. Weak-flying birds such as domestic chickens have a relatively poor blood supply to breast muscles, as one can see from the pale color of the flesh. Strong fliers have good circulation in these muscles and an additional pigment called myoglobin in the cells to facilitate respiration. As a result, the muscle is dark-red in color.

Hawks' eyes are eight to ten times keener than humans'.

Flight demands accurate sight and keen nervous coordination, and birds have both. Their eyes and the optic lobes in the brain are large. The eyeballs do not move as freely as those of mammals, but the flexible neck more than makes up for this. Hawks and other birds of prey have eyes eight to ten times keener than those of human beings. This does not mean that hawks have eyes like telescopes, but that the eye is constructed for greater efficiency. At the most sensitive parts of the retina of a hawk's eye, the foveae—the rods and cones—are packed in at numbers up to 1.5 million. Comparing the equivalent part of a man's eye, we count only 200,000 visual cells. This gives a hawk tremendous advantage in distinguishing tiny details.

A bird's feathers make him more efficient in the air than any airplane. Feathers are structured for protection against heat and cold, for fanning the air, and for streamlining the body. Every slight change of

Above: ground squirrel as seen by human eyes. Below: a hawk's-eye view of the same squirrel.

position of a feather during flight is designed to extract energy from the air and use it effectively. For their weight, feathers are stronger than any man-made substitute. A domestic hen can claim more than 8,300, while a swan sports 25,200 (four fifths of them on the head and neck). A ruby-throated hummingbird has only 940, but it boasts more feathers per square inch than the swan.

Look at the construction of a single wing feather under a microscope, and you will see one of the most marvelous sights in all of nature. Compared to the relatively simple scutes of reptiles and scales of other creatures, a bird's feather is superior in design and function. A single wing feather of a pigeon consists of more than *a million* parts!

Along both sides of the stiff quill (rachis) are grooves which bear filamentous barbs, forming the flat vanes of the feather. There are usually several hundred barbs in each vane, held together by tiny barbules, which in turn bear flanges and minute hooks called hamuli. These parts work together like a zipper. When these become unzipped, the bird zips them up again by preening. Next time you find a feather, run your fingers over the vanes toward the thick end of the quill. The flanges and hooks will separate and the barbs will look ragged and tattered. Now zip the feather parts together again by slipping the vanes between your fingers toward the tip of the feather. You may have to try several times before you make the feather look neat again.

Under the microscope, a wing feather is seen as one of the most marvelous sights in all of nature. A single wing feather of a pigeon consists of more than a million parts. Left: (A) a bird's feather showing (B) arrangement of shaft (rachis), barbs, and barbules; and (C) hooks (hamuli) which simulate zipper action.

Right: barbs and barbules of an eagle's wing feather; hooks on barbules; and the same parts under greater magnification.

Birds' wings automatically adjust to every slight change in air flow. A minor shift in two key feathers would ground a bird.

A feather's design automatically changes its shape during flight in response to different pressures from the air. The rachis (quill) may be curved or straight. The feather itself may be thick or thin, round and hollow, square or polyhedral (many-sided), flat or grooved, depending upon air pressure.

Efficient prolonged flight can occur only when every slight change in airflow is automatically compensated by the feathered wings. The flight feathers of the wingtip, like the propeller of an airplane, are mobile and variable in pitch to cope with the changing stresses of the air. The base acts like the wing of a plane, and the secondary and tertiary wing feathers function as the ailerons and flaps. A slight change in the position or shape of two key primary feathers would ground a bird.

On the leading edge of a bird's wing is the alula, a special aileron consisting of three feathers. This serves to form a wing slot during slow expert maneuvering in a small space. The flight feathers of the wing also slot to prevent stalling, or to lower the stalling speed. The tail serves as both rudder and elevators. Birds such as the puffins, guillemots, and murres have very short tails. To compensate, their webbed feet extend beyond the tail, acting as rudders and elevators by tilting and spreading the extended webs.

Sensory receptors record the precise position of each feather and effect fine adjustments of 12,000 tiny muscles.

Embedded in the skin near the quill of each flight feather are nerve endings which convert the feathers into sensory receptors. These record the precise position of each feather, and through intimate connections with reflex arcs in the spinal cord, effect

The alula (arrow) serves as a slot to reduce turbulence and facilitate reduced landing speed. (1) Normal airplane wing position; (2) stall, with turbulence; (3) slot solves the problem.

Canada geese in flight show down stroke that produces lift and forward thrust; and upstroke, a quick backward flip with partly folded wings.

the continuous variations and fine adjustments of more than 12,000 tiny muscles attached to the bases of the feathers.

The exact body position of the bird is recorded by semicircular canals in the inner ear, which report the changing conditions to the cerebellum of the bird's brain. The cerebellum in birds is better developed than in most other creatures, containing great numbers of sensory fibers which receive transmissions of muscle tensions from the body and wings. The assembled messages spark back to give the bird split-second coordination.

Different species can be identified by their flight characteristics. A crow does not fly like a blue jay. A titmouse does not fly like a woodpecker. A mallard does not fly like a teal. Ornithologists recognize four main kinds of flight: power flying, gliding, soaring, and special flight patterns.

To develop lift and forward thrust, the feathers twist at an angle to the direction of motion.

In flapping or power flight, the downstroking wings develop lift and forward thrust. To accomplish this, the primary feathers twist at an angle to the direction of motion. Air resistance to the wing propels the bird forward. The secondary wing feathers balance the downward pull of the primaries to produce horizontal motion. In other words, the rotation of the outer primaries and the adjustments of the secondaries give a level forward thrust. The upstroke, a quick backward flip with partly folded wings, lifts and thrusts the bird forward.

Generally, the larger the bird the slower it flaps its wings. A hummingbird vibrates its wings about fifty times a second, a heron only twice.

Gliding flight is something like tobogganing downhill. Giant albatrosses, wings spanning up to twelve feet, use this type of flight. They glide for hours over the surface of the sea, rarely flapping their wings. A good glider travels the longest distance possible horizontally with the smallest possible loss of height. Flight efficiency depends on the shape of the wings and the angle which the surface of the wings creates with its own direction of motion. The speed of the glide is limited by the size of the wings and the weight of the bird. A light bird with large wings glides slowly, while a heavy bird with small wings develops greater speed.

Sustained gliding flight depends also on the motion of the air. If the air is motionless the glider must eventually reach the surface of the earth or water, the duration depending on the height from which the glide began. Upward air currents over the troughs and crests of waves, however, sustain the long flights of shearwaters and albatrosses at sea.

Making use of upward air currents, gliding birds "toboggan" on air, but rise if currents are strong enough.

A shearwater glides down an air slope, losing vertical altitude at ten feet per second. But an equivalent upward air current will cause the bird to glide in level flight. If the air rises from the water surface faster than the rate of the bird's glide, the bird without effort will gain altitude. When the wind speed equals the forward and downward speed of the bird, its ground speed will be zero and the bird will appear to be suspended absolutely still in the air. Like a man walking down an upgoing escalator at the same speed, he goes nowhere.

15

Birds "toboggan" on air like playful otters sliding down a snowbank.

Some birds seem to glide about for sheer pleasure on windy days. A few years ago I watched some gulls hover in the breeze above the high point of a rocky island off the west coast of North America. At the highest point stood a lighthouse capped with a slender spire. Several gulls took turns circling, hovering near, and holding the tip of the spire with their bills. When one lost the grip the next in line would move in to hang on. Nearby some guillemots, which have short wings and normally do not glide, circled over the crest of the rocky peaks, laboring slowly against the stiff breezes, then turned to glide down the lee side like playful otters sliding on snow. But the guillemots tobogganed on air.

Land birds such as buzzards, hawks, and eagles soar in great circles, gradually attaining great heights, then dive swiftly downward to start another spiral. They ride the thermal upcurrents until they reach a downdraft which enables them to reach high speeds without ever flapping their wings.

The bird progresses by expending only a minimum of energy. Everyone has at some time seen birds soaring with their wingtips spread like fingers on a hand. Called slotting, this function prevents air turbulence behind the wings when the wings are tilted downward at the trailing edge. A bird slots its wings when it flies at reduced speeds or lands.

Hummingbirds' wings function like the rotors of a helicopter.

The extremely complicated patterns of coordination and motion involved in vertical, reverse, and hovering flight—helicopter actions—of swifts, hummingbirds, and skylarks are not fully understood by scientists. These acrobats not only use a powered downstroke but also a powered upstroke.

Unlike other birds, the hummingbird flies almost exclusively with its hands, the elbow permanently bent. The shoulder

Buzzards, hawks, and eagles soar in great circles, riding thermal upcurrents, then dive swiftly only to start another spiral. They attain high speeds without flapping wings.

Hummingbirds' wings, though they operate backward and forward, perform like rotors of a helicopter. The wings are attached to the shoulder by a swivel joint, and the wing-beat rate varies little in flight. Hummingbirds' complicated wing movements make possible vertical, reverse, and hovering flight.

Above: The owl, a master of silent flight, glides effortlessly through the night searching for prey.

Left: A chickadee "slots" its wings as it comes in for a landing.

joint is motile, making the hummingbird highly maneuverable. In some ways a hummingbird's wings are like the wings of insects. They operate backward and forward in a rowing motion, but they also tilt like the wings of a dragonfly or the rotors of a helicopter.

No matter what maneuver this bird makes, the wing-beat rate varies no more than 5 percent. The average wing beat remains at about fifty-two times per second for the female rubythroat, regardless of her flight motion. By using a simple mathematical formula, Crawford H. Greenewalt, an authority on hummingbirds, predicted the wing-beat rate of a flying animal, determined by the rate of wing beat and its length and the size of the flying animal. For example, by knowing that an insect has a wing length of seven millimeters and a wing-beat rate of 500 per second, we can calculate that a bird with a wing length 100 times as great will beat its wings 1.5 times per second.

The phenomenon of bird flight is so intricate that its origin must lie, not in chance, but in the intelligence of the Creator.

A bird flying, propelling itself by its own coordinated muscular efforts, is surely one of Nature's masterpieces. To me, the whole phenomenon of bird flight is so fantastically intricate that I can only conclude that its origin must lie, not in the realm of haphazard chance, but in the intelligence of the Designer and Creator.

Thirty centuries ago David, poet-king of the Hebrews, sighed, "Oh, that I had wings like a dove! . . . then would I fly away." Solomon, the wise man, likewise amazed, exclaimed, "The way of an eagle in the air" is "too wonderful for me."

It is "too wonderful" for me also. And I believe it is "too wonderful" for blind chance as well. "Too wonderful," indeed, for anyone or anything except the great Designer, the Creator.

Two streamlined swallows in effortless flight. Since ancient times human beings have envied the birds' ability to fly.

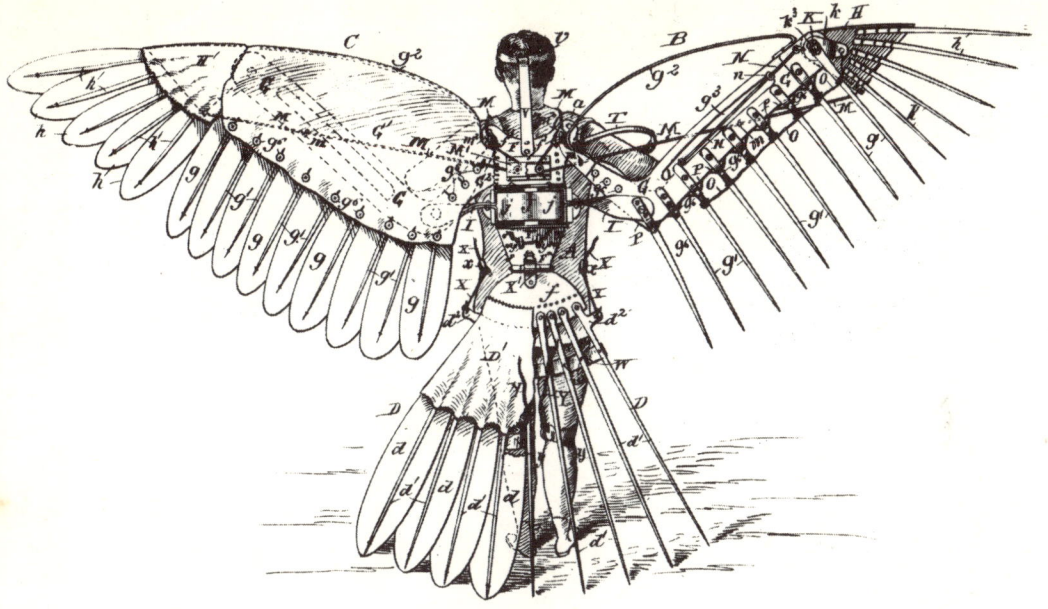

Early attempts to imitate the birds produced many a weird, clumsy contraption, and some serious falls. R. J. Spalding's set of wings and tail (above) was actually patented on March 5, 1889, but of course never left the ground. Darius Green (left), aviation pioneer, made batlike wings and jumped from a barn window. Forlini of Italy and Delprad of Germany tried out an early form of autogiro (below, left) in 1894. The inventors called the machine "Bird Generator Motor Propeller," but the public labeled it as "a blend of bat and dragon." W. F. Quimby (left) tried to fly by attaching birdlike wings to arms and legs. A contemporary of Quimby's commented: "We hardly think he will be able to compete with the swallows, and would advise him to start from some low point at first, so that if he should fall down it will not hurt so much."

23

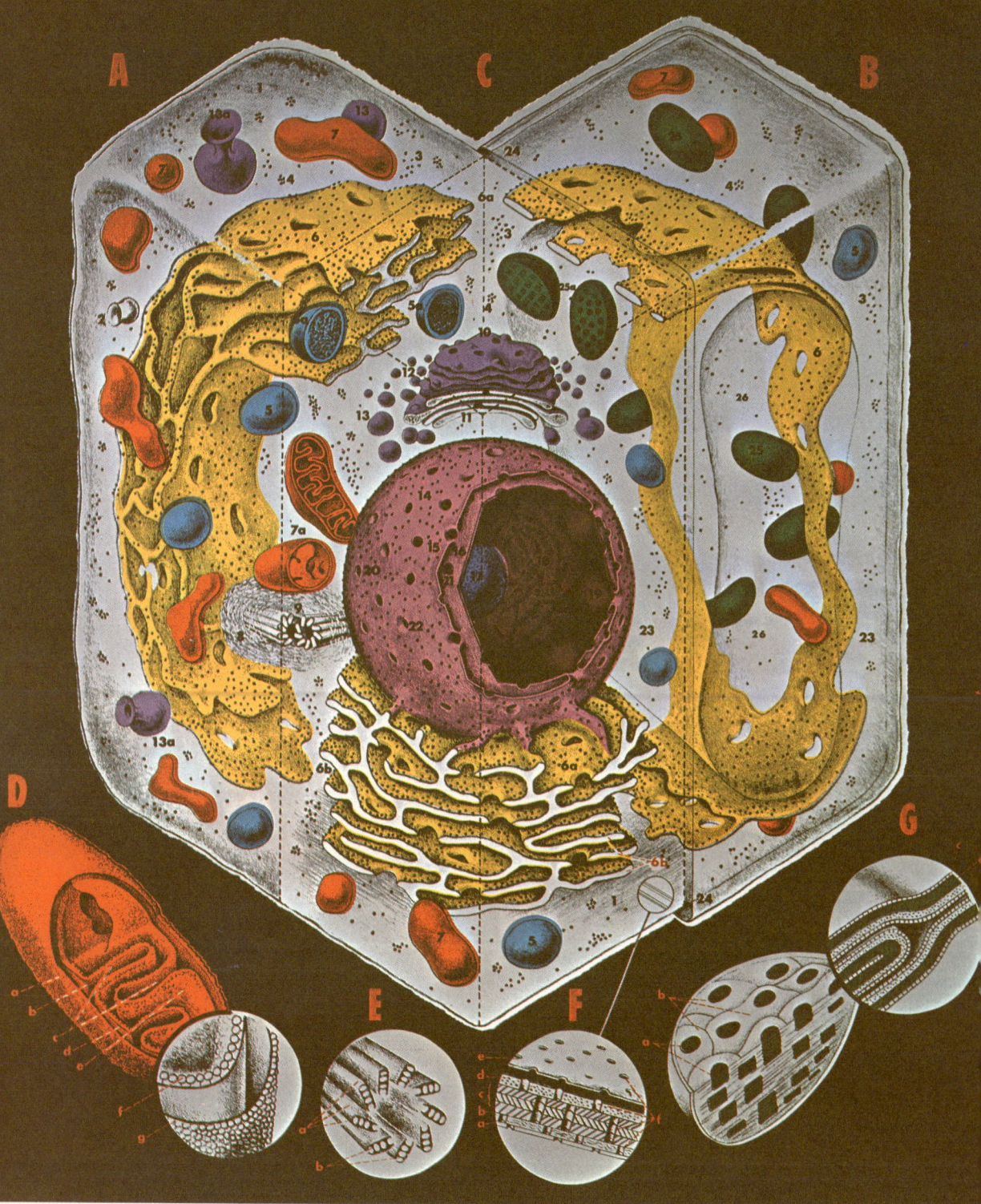

A. Animal cell.
B. Plant cell.
C. Structures in both animal and plant cells.
  1. Cell membrane (double). Desmosomes, the structures that bond contiguous cells together, are not shown.
  2. Pinocytic vesicle (inpouching cell membrane).
  3. Ribosomes. These occur on the surface of the endoplasmic reticulum, on the outer nuclear membrane, on the nucleolus, and free throughout the cytoplasm.
  4. Polyribosomes.
  5. Lysosomes.
  5a. Lysosomes in section.
  6. Endoplasmic reticulum, rough surfaced. (Smooth endoplasmic reticulum is seen only in certain kinds of specialized cells.)
  6a. Endoplasmic reticulum sectioned to show lumens.
  6b. Lumens of endoplasmic reticulum.
  7. Mitochondria (chondriosomes).
  7a. Mitochondria in section.
  8. Centrosphere.
  9. Centrioles. According to most recent findings, these bodies appear to consist of nine bundles of tubules—not eleven bundles.
  10. Golgi apparatus.
  11. Golgi apparatus, flattened vesicles.
  12. Golgi apparatus, microvesicles.
  13. Golgi apparatus, secretory vesicles.
  13a. Golgi apparatus. Secretory vesicle products leaving the cell.
  14. Nucleus.
  15. Nuclear membrane, outer.
  16. Nuclear membrane, inner.
  17. Nucleolus.
  18. Nuclear chromatin.
  19. Nucleoplasm.
  20. Pores in outer nuclear membrane.
  21. Pores in inner nuclear membrane.
  22. Nuclear pores, continuous through both nuclear membranes, permit exchange between nucleoplasm and cytoplasm. According to some authorities, these openings are fenestra.
  23. Cytoplasm.
  24. Plant cell wall.
  25. Chloroplast.
  25a. Chloroplast sectioned to show lateral and surface views of grana.
  26. Vacuole.
D. Mitochondrion, enlarged and sectioned to expose internal details.
  a. Outer membrane.
  b. Inner membrane.
  c. Cristae.
  d. Infrastructure space.
  e. Interstructure space. (Insert—fine structure of mitochondrion.)
  f. Mitochondrial subunits on short stalks. These structures are concerned with electron transfer leading to adenosine triphosphate (ATP) synthesis.
  g. Mitochondrial subunits, stalkless. These units are concerned with oxidation reactions that supply electrons to the interior.
E. Centriole, details of.
  a. Bundles (total of nine bundles).
  b. Tubules (as many as three to a bundle).
F. Plant cell wall, sectioned.
  a. Middle lamella.
  b. Primary wall.
  c. Secondary wall.
  d. Tertiary lamella.
  e. Cell membrane (double).
  f. Pores (plasmodesmata).
G. Chloroplast, sectioned and enlarged.
  a. Grana. These are stacks of chlorophyll discs. A granum consists of one stack of discs.
  b. Stroma lamella.
     (Insert—fine structure of sectioned disc of granum—hypothetical.)
  c. Protein layer (vertical hatching).
  d. Chlorophyll layer (diagonal hatching).
  e. Lipid layer (dotted).

2. Inside a "Simple" Cell

Joan Beltz Roberts

"Look at this," the professor exclaimed, drawing a tiny circle on the blackboard. "This is a cell."

I was attending a class in plant physiology taught by Dr. Richard Belkengren, at Oregon State University. He had a way of reciting 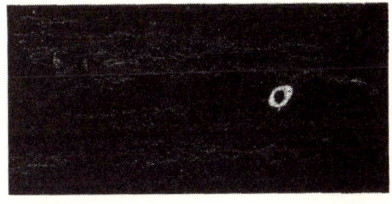 long, impressive lists, and the one he gave us that day was impressive indeed. "Just one simple cell, and look what it can do," he said.

For emphasis he jabbed at that poor little cell with his chalk and began to enumerate:

1. It can take in nutrients (food), first "deciding" which nutrients to take and which ones to reject.

2. It can absorb or give off water according to its needs.

3. It can manufacture all the materials of which it is made.

4. It can put those materials together in proper fashion to construct a new cell.

5. It can harness the energy needed for all of its activities.

6. It can store energy, raw materials, and finished products for future use.

7. In many cases it can manufacture chemicals to be used elsewhere, such as antibiotics and exoenzymes.

8. It can give off these chemicals, along with waste materials.

The professor paused for breath, then added, "This is where the evolutionists begin, with the cell. The time scale of evolutionary development can be illustrated roughly by this line, from the first primordial cell to the complex living things we see today." He drew a line fifteen or twenty inches long.

"But the real story, the one we ought to be studying, the one we know nothing at all about, is the story represented by *this* line."

Returning to the tiny cell on the board, he drew a line *backward,* to the end of the blackboard, across the wall, past the door, and, with a flourish, all the way around the room.

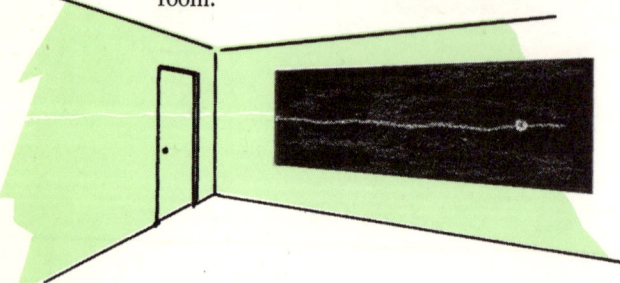

"There!" he said triumphantly. "There's the real evolution. There's where the real mysteries are."

Protoplasm has one of the most complicated and beautiful structures in the universe.

"Protoplasm (cell material) has one of the most complicated and beautiful structures in the universe," writes Rutherford Platt. "So elaborate are cells that one can say that nature had already done most of her job by the time she evolved them. After that it was merely a matter of putting cells together to build fishes, birds, horses, elephants—even human beings."[1]

Before we try to describe the first, or "primordial" cell, let us look into a "typical" cell of today and notice the processes going on there which are common to all cells. Then we will try to see which of these processes would have had to be present in that first bit of living matter.

Every living cell has a thin covering called the plasma membrane. But this is more than a mere covering; it is a complex living thing. It is made of two fatty layers sandwiched between two layers of protein molecules.

Membranes "decide" which substances enter and leave cell.

Somehow this membrane "decides" what substances will enter the cell, which ones will leave, and the exact amounts of the materials entering and leaving. This is not a simple action like a sieve letting small particles pass while retaining the larger ones. A cell membrane is highly selective. It permits free passage of some particles, one-way traffic for others, and no passage at all for still others. Some particles seem to move by simple diffusion through pores in the membrane, just as cooking aromas pass from room to room until they permeate the house. Other particles apparently are pumped in or out. Potassium is concentrated inside the cell, while sodium is usually refused entrance or else is pumped

1. Excerpts from "The Wondrous 'Inner Space' of Living Cells," by Rutherford Platt, *The Reader's Digest,* June, 1964.

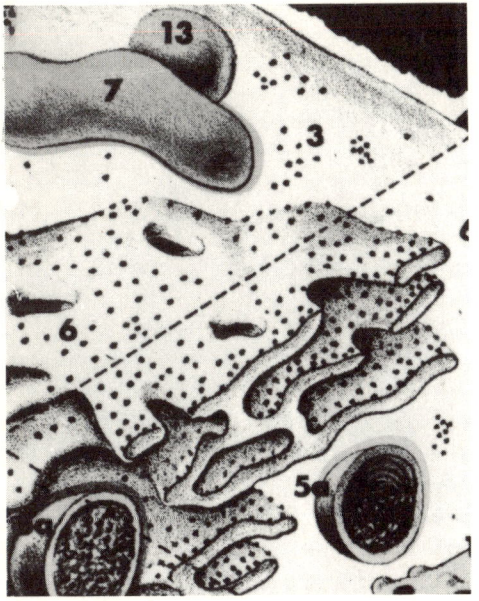

Cell parts: (3) ribosomes (5a) lysosomes in section (6) endoplasmic reticulum (7) mitochondria (13) Golgi apparatus.

COURTESY CCM: GENERAL BIOLOGICAL, INC.: CHICAGO

out as fast as it enters. The cells of the kidney tubules pump in one direction some substances which the body needs to keep, and at the same time pump in the opposite direction other substances which are to be excreted.

How does this membrane perform so many tasks at the same time?

Some materials are actually engulfed by the membrane and drawn into the cell by a remarkable process called "cellular drinking." The cell membrane sends out fingerlike projections which curl toward one another and join, enclosing a droplet of water which contains food material. Or the membrane may simply dimple inward, carrying with it the desired droplet. Whichever happens, the food becomes enclosed in a tiny membranous sac which slowly moves inward, detaches itself from the cell membrane, and becomes a part of the interior of the cell. Electron microscope studies have followed the process this far, but no one knows what happens next. The forces which cause the cell membrane to behave in this mysterious way are also unknown.

Within the main body of the cell is another membrane, a double one, which is stretched, twisted, contorted, joined, separated, and rejoined. Anyone who has ever tried to follow the twists and turns of a commercial fisherman's net or straighten out a sheet of used plastic wrap, or even refold a large highway map, still has only an inkling of the complexity of this membrane, called the endoplasmic reticulum, ER for short. Probably the space between the two layers of the ER is actually a system of canals, used to transport materials from one place to another within the cell. Some of these canals lead into the nucleus and some lead out to the exterior of the cell.

But so far we are describing only the gross structure of the ER. Even this can be seen only with the help of an electron microscope, and in viewing the ER one may think that he has, at last, probed the cell's most intimate secrets. Yet this membrane, which looks like a simple sheet, must have a fine structure which we have not even begun to perceive. Otherwise how could it perform so many varied tasks, and do them all at the same time? How does the plasma membrane selectively move materials into the cell or out of it? How does ER transport materials about within the cell? How does it "decide" which materials to transport and in what direction?

Perhaps one day we shall see these wonderful little factories where protein building occurs.

On the surface of the membranes making up the ER, tiny granules called ribosomes may be found. These are actually factories within which protein molecules are assembled. In fact, each ribosome appears to be a miniature assembly line which receives its instructions directly from the nucleus.

So far we have seen the ribosomes only as tiny granules. Yet these, too, must have structure in order for them to perform as assembly lines, for messenger molecules of RNA (ribonucleic acid) travel from the nucleus to the ribosomes. No one has yet explained the forces guiding or propelling the RNA.

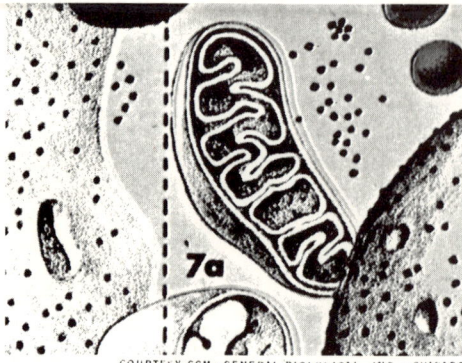
COURTESY CCM: GENERAL BIOLOGICAL, INC.: CHICAGO

Having arrived at their destination, these messenger RNA molecules somehow find their proper positions. Then somehow amino acids from other parts of the cell are brought to the ribosomes where they are joined together, following the pattern imprinted in the structure of the RNA, to make protein molecules. Perhaps one day we shall discover a way to "look," at least with the mind's eye, into these wonderful little factories and to understand exactly where and how this process of protein building takes place. Will we then find that even the ribosome is made up of still smaller units?

Mitochondria, manufacturing ATP, the power molecules, are the "powerhouses" of the cell.

The cell matter also contains egg-shaped bodies called mitochondria. These also are formed of double membranes, the inner membrane folded neatly within a little membranous sac. The surfaces of these inner membranes again seem to serve as tiny assembly lines or, in this case, disassembly lines. For there, electrons move from one enzyme molecule to another in a precise and orderly way. As they travel, they lend their energy to a series of chemical reactions which result in the formation of molecules of ATP (adenosine triphosphate), a remarkable substance which provides the energy to run many of the cell's activities. The electrons, when they reach the end of the line, unite with oxygen and hydrogen to form water.

Because they manufacture ATP, the power molecules, the mitochondria are frequently called the powerhouses of the cell.

No one has seen mitochondria within bacterial cells, but research has shown that the assembly line is present and functioning. The bacterial powerhouse appears to be an organized system of enzymes, though we have not yet discovered exactly how it is arranged or what keeps the enzymes in their proper order.

Another structure found within most cells is the Golgi body, an arrangement of concave double membranes, set one within the other like a stack of mixing bowls. Golgi bodies are both factories and transport systems. They manufacture or at least assemble materials such as hormones and enzymes which the cell secretes.

The Golgi bodies are always present in actively secreting cells. In pancreatic cells they contain digestive enzymes; in the thyroid gland they enclose thyroid hormone; in the developing sperm they specialize in an enzyme which will dissolve a pathway through the materials around the egg to give the sperm access to the egg surface. Just how the different Golgi bodies receive their instructions is as mysterious as the way they perform their various tasks.

The Golgi bodies even travel about in the cell to accomplish their different tasks. For example, in the ovary the follicle cells have two separate duties: They secrete yolk material into the egg, and they secrete the hormone estrogen into a space where it can be picked up by the bloodstream. During the yolk-secreting period the Golgi bodies take their places on the side of the cell nearest the developing egg. Then, when it is time to begin estrogen production, they move to the opposite side of the cell.

A single cell, kept alive in a nutrient medium, can grow a new plant complete with roots, leaves, and flowers.

The activities of the cell are governed from the main executive offices, found in the nucleus. This is usually located near the center. Here are the chromosomes, which contain the information that determines the activities of the cell, plus the information needed to build a complete new cell when necessary. Further, the chromosomes within every single cell of many-celled organisms store information which is used only under unusual circumstances—the information needed to build a complete new body, with its many different kinds of cells. Scientists have taken a single cell from the stem of a tobacco plant, and simply by keeping it alive in a nutrient medium, grown from that one cell a new plant complete with roots, leaves, and flowers! Experiments of this kind have also been performed with carrot and parsley cells. Of course, this phenomenon is also seen in the process of sexual reproduction, in which

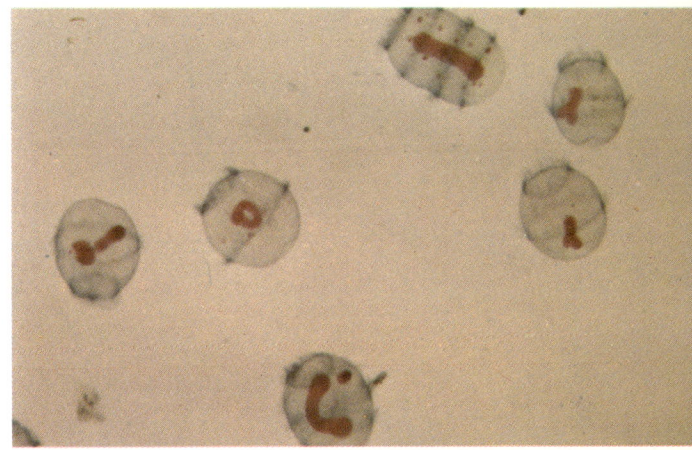

COURTESY CCM: GENERAL BIOLOGICAL, INC.: CHICAGO

Above: The didinium is an aggressive little protozoan hunter, who eats up to eight paramecia per day.

Below: cells divide in order to multiply. Here whitefish mitosis is in progress, with mitotic figures ranging from metaphase through late anaphase. Photograph magnification 500 times.

COURTESY CCM: GENERAL BIOLOGICAL, INC.: CHICAGO

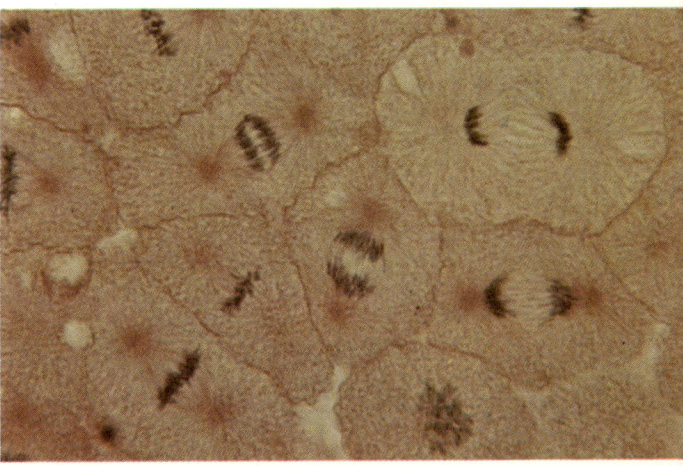

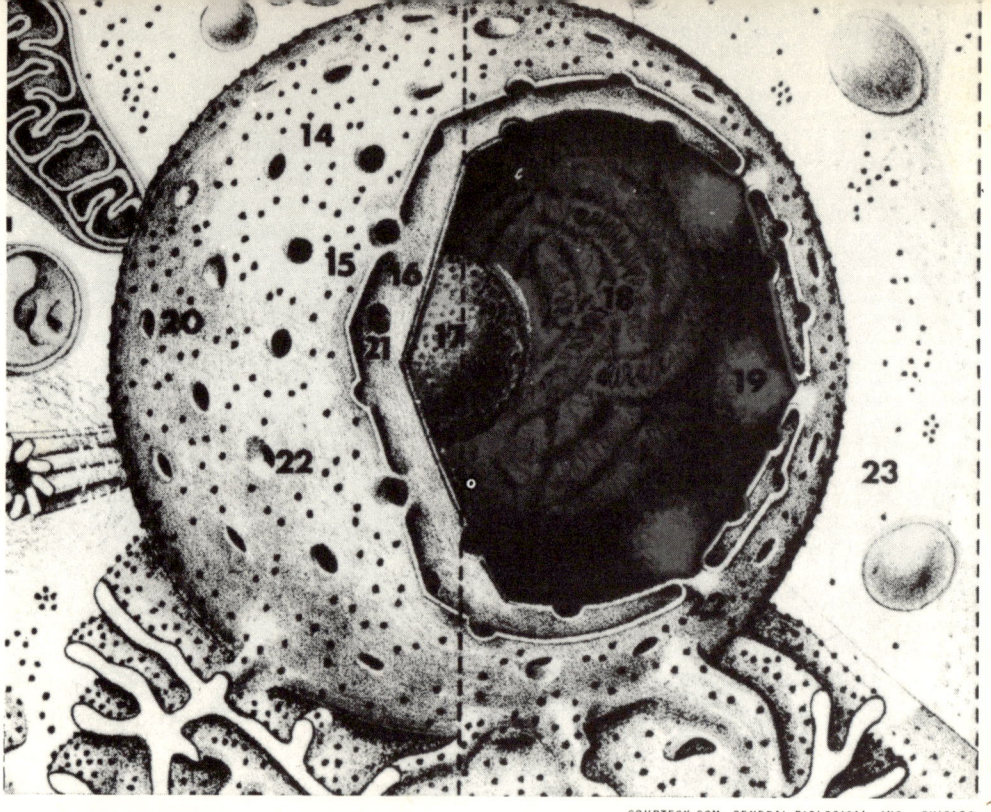

COURTESY CCM: GENERAL BIOLOGICAL, INC.: CHICAGO

The cell's "headquarters"
is the nucleus, with
its many functions.

(15) The nucleus.

(16) Outer nuclear membrane.

(17) Nucleolus.

(18) Nuclear chromatin.

(19) Nucleoplasm.

(20-22) Pores.

(23) Cytoplasm.

the egg and sperm unite to form a single cell whose chromosomes contain the information necessary to produce a complete new organism.

The nucleus, therefore, does three things. It governs the day-to-day activities of the cell by sending instructions to the ribosomes, ordering the specific proteins to be manufactured. It also, in some way we do not yet understand, governs cell division. The chromosomes are able to duplicate themselves so that each of the two daughter cells receives a complete set of the information stored in the original cell. And finally, the nucleus governs the development of the cell, determining whether it becomes muscle, bone, nerve, or skin.

This information is stored in the chromosomes in the form of molecules called deoxyribonucleic acid (DNA). The complicated structure of this molecule was finally worked out by two scientists, Watson and Crick, who won the Nobel Prize in 1962 for their achievement.

DNA is a huge molecule (as molecules go) made up of repeating subunits called deoxyribotides, which are themselves ex-

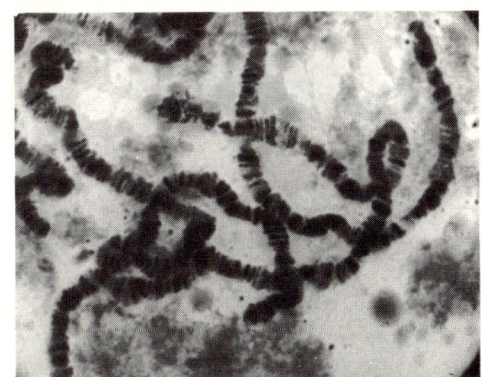

Chromosomes from the salivary gland of a drosophila, or fruit fly. Chromosomes contain the information needed to produce a complete new organism.

COURTESY CCM: GENERAL BIOLOGICAL, INC.: CHICAGO

ceedingly complex. The subunits are of four different varieties, and can be combined in various proportions and in different orders. Theoretically there is an almost infinite variety of DNA molecules.

Two amazing things about the DNA molecule are that it can duplicate itself, and that it can direct the production of messenger RNA molecules which carry the information from the nucleus out to the cytoplasm (the principal cell fluid). The RNA, then, carries instructions from the executive offices to the assembly line, directing the manufacture of body chemicals.

Some cells are specialized; some are both "jack of all trades" and master of all of them.

RNA, before it is sent from the nucleus out into the cytoplasm, is believed to be stored in a small structure called the nucleolus, seen on the surface of the nucleus. Observers have actually seen the nucleolus in living cells enlarge, then squeeze down, apparently squirting its contents out into the cytoplasm. In addition, pores have been discovered in the nuclear membrane; not just holes, but little depressions covered over with a very thin film. Their function is unknown, but these pores may affect the passage of materials into the nucleus or out of it. Thus the RNA is dispatched from the nucleus out into the cytoplasm, traveling by way of the nucleolus, or through the pores in the nuclear membrane, or perhaps by some route no one has yet discovered.

A cell can become specialized to perform certain functions only if it is supported by other cells that can take over other necessary tasks. In a community of human beings, no person can devote all his time to building houses unless someone else nearby grows food and prepares clothing. So, in a many-celled organism, which is really a community of cells, there is a division of labor and the cells become specialized.

Let us now take a look at some one-celled creatures that live independently of other cells. One would think that such a cell would have to be a "jack of all trades and master of none." This independent cell is indeed a jack of all trades, but if it is

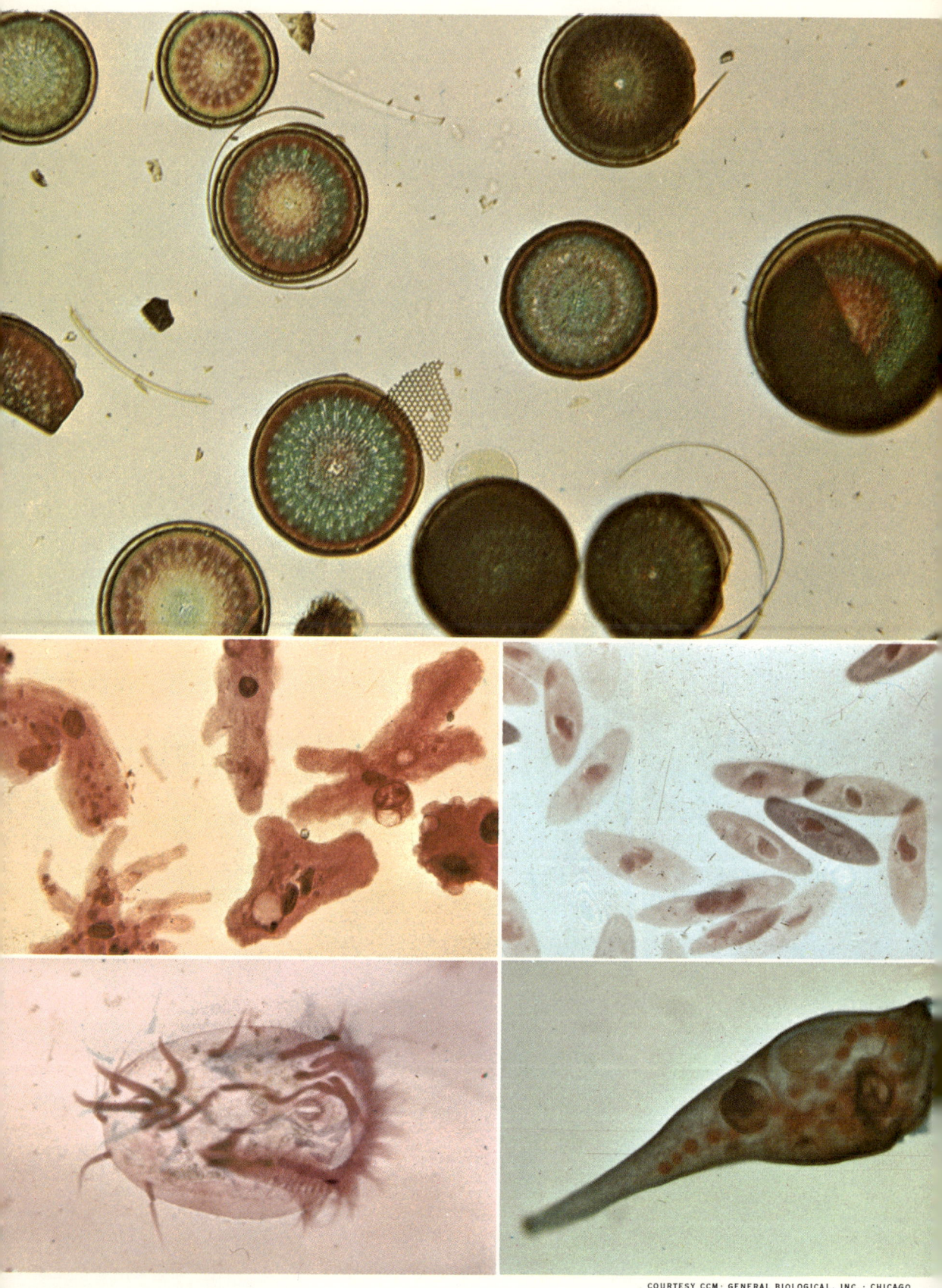

COURTESY CCM: GENERAL BIOLOGICAL, INC.: CHICAGO

Diatoms (above, left) are microscopic algae found in abundance in fresh and salt water. They have hard silicified cell walls which remain when they die as "diatomaceous earth."
The amoeba (middle, left) is a single-celled but complex protozoan which can move about, seek and engulf food particles, respond to light and darkness, and reproduce its kind. Other protozoa are the paramecium and (lower, left to right) euplotes and stentor.

to survive it must also be master of all of them!

The amoeba—more complex than a highly diversified factory.

One of the simpler one-celled animals is the amoeba. Here is what appears to be a mere blob of cell fluid enclosed in a plasma membrane, containing one or more nuclei. Actually it is more complex than a highly diversified factory, though on a minute scale. It is able to move about; to seek, recognize, and engulf food particles; to digest and assimilate this food; to respond to light and darkness; and to reproduce its own kind. In addition, some amoebas produce remarkable shells about themselves; only a few species are naked. These shells are protective and highly decorative. See the illustrations of foraminifera and radiolaria.

Other one-celled animals and plants also manufacture intricately ornamented cell walls, some of which are shown in the illustrations of dinoflagellates, diatoms, and algae.

Many one-celled organisms swim about by moving short appendages called cilia. The paramecium is a well-known example. The paramecium, somewhat oval in shape, looks simple enough. It is covered with cilia and has a groove leading to the "mouth" where food particles are taken in. But a closer look shows that the surface of the cell has an elaborate pattern delicately inscribed upon it.

The cilia—a study in control and co-ordination.

What kind of mechanism coordinates the cilia with one another in their movements? Why do the cilia beat so gracefully? Why do they not thrash about at random? If they did, they would be worthless; the paramecium could not use them to move about. Some orderly system of control must be in operation here, and its discovery is one of the challenges of modern science.

The cilia, when viewed with an electron microscope, are seen to be wonderfully complex, as shown in the electron micrograph. Incidentally, this structural pattern is seen in most cilia and flagella (whip-shaped cilia), as well as in the tail of the sperm, the "hairs" of olfactory sensory cells, and, surprisingly, in the rods and cones which are the light receptors in the eyes of men and animals.

Another simple creature, the didinium, uses two rings of cilia to move around. Didinium is an aggressive little hunter with its snout on its back. It sticks out the snout, attaches it to its prey, then retracts the snout and draws the victim into its body and digests it. Its favorite meal is the paramecium; the didinium will eat as many as eight in one day, even though the hunter is much smaller than the prey.

Two of the simplest kinds of plant cells carry on all the complicated life processes.

Two of the very simplest plant groups, the bacteria and the blue-green algae, have cells which may lack some of the membranous structures other cells have. Thus the nuclear material is much more difficult to distinguish from the rest of the cell. Still, these simple cells carry on all the complicated life processes; there must be a separate "room" for each different type of activity. The nucleus keeps its identity, and the cell processes take place in an orderly way. We don't know many of the details as yet; nevertheless these organisms function effectively.

Blue-green algae glide about, and respond to sunlight.

These simplest cells must have some means of separating their various chemical activities, for some processes involve chemicals that would destroy other processes. For example, in the nucleus the components of RNA are joined together to make the large RNA molecule. This chemical reaction is aided by the presence of an enzyme, RNA polymerase. However, enzymes usually help reactions to take place in both directions. That is, the enzyme can cause the raw materials to combine into RNA molecules, *and,* if the RNA remains in the vicinity, the same enzyme will take them apart again. So, if the RNA is to remain intact, it has to be shipped out of the nucleus at once. This seems to be the purpose of the nucleolus—to provide a safe place for temporary storage of RNA molecules.

Even these "simple" cells show some remarkable complexities. Bacteria may have flagella, arranged in patterns. Each flagellum consists of a core surrounded by coiled

---

What kind of mechanism coordinates the cilia with one another in their movements? Why do the cilia beat so gracefully? Why do they not thrash about at random? If they did, they would be worthless; the paramecium could not use them to move about. Some orderly system of control must be in operation here, and its discovery is one of the challenges of modern science.

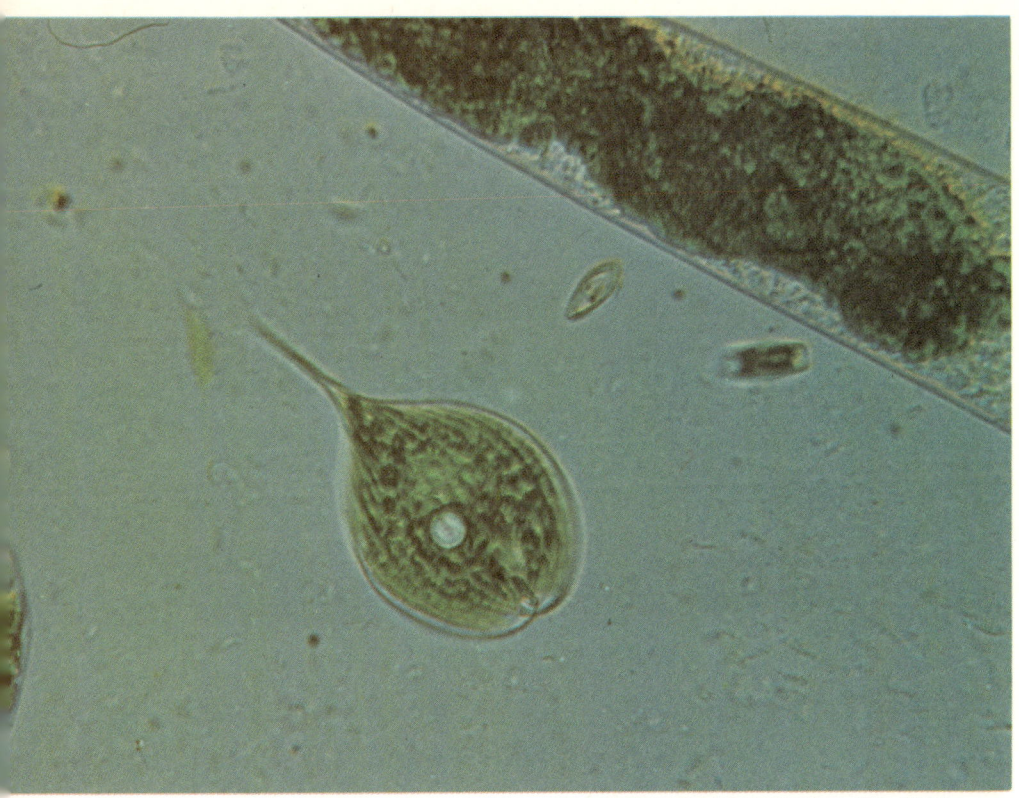

Examples of blue-green algae are the phacus and (below) rivularia. These simple plants move about and respond to light.

COURTESY CCM: GENERAL BIOLOGICAL, INC.: CHICAGO

threadlike fibrils. Some bacteria are tiny spheres, while others resemble stalks or long corkscrews.

Blue-green algae come in many shapes and sizes. Some of them, such as Oscillatoria and Spirullina, glide about in some mysterious way that no one has yet fully explained. In addition, they can respond to light, choosing to float in the water at the precise depth where light conditions are most nearly ideal. They rise to the surface on cloudy days and sink deep into the water under a blazing noonday sun.

These processes, essential to life, had to occur within the first living "primordial cell."

What processes, then, are carried on within these wonderful structures called cells? A detailed list would be long, but here are a few:
1. Processes involved with getting food —recognizing food materials and taking them into the cell.
2. Processes by which the food is digested, assimilated, and formed into new substances to be used as raw materials.
3. Chemical reactions in which some of these raw materials are transformed into energy, to be used as heat or to run other chemical reactions.
4. Chemical reactions in which raw materials are turned into materials to build the cell—reactions involving growth, repair, secretion, and reproduction.
5. Processes involved with discharging wastes and unwanted by-products from the cell.

All of these processes are essential to life. All of them had to occur within that "primordial" cell which most evolutionists believe was the first living thing.

We have seen something of the structures necessary to carry on these processes. But what of the chemicals needed before these processes could occur? Joshua Lederberg, in his speech of acceptance of the Nobel Prize in 1959, listed the minimum requirements:
1. DNA.
2. An abundance of the four deoxyribotide pyrophosphates.
3. One molecule of DNA polymerase.
4. Ribotide phosphates.
5. One molecule of RNA polymerase.
6. A supply of twenty amino-acyl nucleotides.
7. One molecule of amino-acyl RNA polymerase.

None of the chemicals necessary to cell structure could be effective except in the presence of all the others. No substitutions would be possible.

The list is impressive. The molecules are fantastically complex and are so specific that

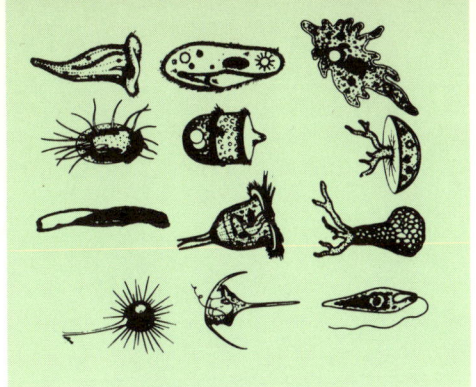

Different types of protozoa, left to right and top to bottom: stentor, paramecium, amoeba, euplotes, didinium, arcella, spirostomum, vorticella, difflugia, aphelota, ceratium (a dinoflagellate), and euglena.

no substitutes will do. No item can be effective except in the presence of all the others.

In addition, these raw materials cannot comprise a living unit so long as they are simply individual molecules floating their separate ways in an organic sea, or even in a test tube. Before such a chemical mixture could be called an organism, it would have to be organized. That is, there must be a structure to enclose the chemicals and put each in its place.

In other words, the raw materials need a factory and some machinery before they can perform any meaningful function. There is not a shred of evidence to suggest that these raw materials are capable of building and equipping their own factory. Of course, once they are established in a factory of their own, they can construct additional factories. This is a large part of the cell's normal work.

The result of unguided evolution or intelligent plan?

Surveying this pageant of living cells one can look at it from various viewpoints. Is it the result of unguided evolutionary processes, possibly suggesting that a law of increasing complexity pervades all nature? Is it the product of an intelligent plan? One need not seek to prove exactly how it came to be. Proof is not the goal of the Christian, nor should it be, for God does not subject Himself to scientific testing by His creatures. It is not seemly—it is not even conceivable—that God should perform at our whim, for this would place creatures in command of their Creator. Also, long past events are generally beyond proof.

We can no longer place our faith in chance events occurring in primeval pools.

But we can accept the present evidence of our senses, together with the instruction given by revelation. The possibility that the ingredients we have described could spontaneously arrange themselves into self-reproducing cells is so incredibly remote that I cannot stretch my faith far enough to believe such a thing. Years ago scientists thought of the cell as a mere blob of jelly. Then it was easy to imagine that the first living cell sprang to life in some warm pool. But now that we know something of the amazing complexity of each tiny cell, we can no longer place such implicit faith in chance events occurring in primeval pools.

The alternative: The "simple" cell, this sophisticated factory, a product of matchless Intellect.

This leads me to the only alternative: This "simple" cell, this highly sophisticated and diversified factory, containing precision machines so delicately tooled and intricately regulated, can only be the product of an incomparable Intellect whom we call God, the Creator.

3. Photosynthesis— Bread From Light

Leonard N. Hare

If you should hike across sizzling Death Valley in mid-July, you might think the big blazing ball in the sky was aiming a lot of its fire directly at you. But this would hardly be true, for the sun squanders most of its energy in empty space. Our planet gets only about one part in 200,000,-000 of the sun's output of light and heat.

Of this tiny fraction of the total, the trees, shrubs, grass, and other plants capture and store only one part in 600. Yet this amount equals all the energy in 300,000,000,000 tons of high-grade coal each year, or 820,000,000 tons a day. We would need 20,500,000 coal cars, each carrying forty tons, to haul a single day's production. With each car forty feet long, the train would stretch for 155,000 miles, more than six times

To haul coal equivalent to the sun's energy captured by earth's plants daily, we would need twenty million coal cars, making a train that circles the globe six times!

around the world at the equator. If this train traveled at sixty miles per hour, and you had to wait at a crossing for it, you would have to be patient for three and one half months until you saw the caboose pass, and could start your motor and be on your way!

The energy represented by the coal in one half of the cars will be used by the plants just to keep growing, and much of the rest is in a form that man cannot use. So a relatively short section of our imaginary train feeds, clothes, and warms all the inhabitants of this earth.

Philosophers of ancient Greece compared a plant's roots, in close contact with the earth, with the mouth of a hungry infant pressed against its mother's breast. The root system reminded them of the infant's mouth, and the earth, of the mother's breast. And what did they compare to the milk? The soil, of course. People thought this way for over fifteen centuries. Then Nicholas of Cusa, who lived 500 years ago, suggested that it is water, rather than soil, that nourishes plants. In 1648 von Helmont thought he had proved this by growing a five-pound willow shoot until it became a 169-pound tree in a tub of soil weighing 200 pounds. During the five years the tree grew, the weight of the soil decreased only two ounces. "Therefore," von Helmont concluded, "164 pounds of wood, bark, and root have arisen from the water alone."

Investigators called the process "photosynthesis"—a putting together with the aid of light.

In 1772 Joseph Priestly of England made a surprising discovery. He found that a sprig of mint not only thrived in air "dephlogisticated"* by combustion or by respiration of animals, but actually restored such air again. Priestly continued his experiments; but he was puzzled, after moving his equipment to a more spacious area away from the window, that he could not repeat his earlier success. Seven years later, Ingen-Housz of Austria, speaking of Priestly's experiment, explained, "This wonderful operation is by no means owing to the vegetation of the plant, but to the influence of the light of the sun upon the plant." He showed that only green plant organs have this capacity. Priestly, he said, should have left his equipment near the window.

*The Phlogiston theory was used by early chemists attempting to explain combustion.

Green predominates in plants because light of other colors is absorbed, while the green is reflected, and thus visible to the eye.

In 1804, a Frenchman by the name of de Saussure made another discovery: "The consumption of carbonic acid gas [carbon dioxide] by leaves is necessary for their existence in the sun." He demonstrated that this gas is consumed and decomposed by green plants exposed to light. The plant absorbs the carbon dioxide and releases oxygen gas to the atmosphere. Later investigators called this process photosynthesis (from *photos,* light, and *synthesis,* putting together) and stated it chemically this way:

$6\,CO_2\ +\ 6\,H_2O\ \rightarrow$
Six carbon dioxide molecules plus six water molecules with sunlight acting on green plant parts,

$C_6H_{12}O_6\ +\ 6\,O_2$
yields one molecule of sugar (glucose) and releases six molecules of oxygen.

When light passes through a prism, it breaks up into wavelengths—the familiar colors of the rainbow. Does each of these colors have the same effect in photosynthesis? In 1887 Englemann shined a light on filaments of blue-green algae with oxygen-loving bacteria on them. When white light shone on the filaments, the bacteria stayed along the entire filament. But when he passed the light through a prism first, the bacteria gathered only on the parts of the filament bathed in blue and red rays. This experiment showed that photosynthesis takes place thanks chiefly to red and blue light waves.

Photosynthesis can be demonstrated by a simple experiment.

If we pass a beam of white light through a solution of the green chlorophyll in ether, then through a prism, we will see that most of the red and blue parts of the spectrum are missing. This means that red and blue light was absorbed by the chlorophyll. In fact, this is why chlorophyll is green. Green light is *not* absorbed, but reflected, by chlorophyll. This is why the trees, grass, and other plant life that cover so much of our world are predominantly green.

We can easily show that chlorophyll is involved in photosynthesis. The leaf of a showy Coleus plant has four colors. It is green on the outer edge, brown nearer in, pink near the center, and white at the very center. When we boil the leaf in water for a few minutes, a pigment is leached out of the leaf, leaving only the green and white. We can see that the original four colors came from just two pigments. If we now boil the leaf in alcohol, the green chlorophyll will be washed out, and the leaf is all white. If we then wash our leaf with a weak iodine solution, the area formerly occupied by the chlorophyll turns a dark blue.

What does this mean? The blue reaction to iodine means starch is present. Where did the starch come from? We know that photosynthesis makes the sugar called glucose ($C_6H_{12}O_6$). When enough of this sugar is present in a cell engaged in photosynthesis, the sugar units are linked together into long chains and become starch. Starch in the leaf cells means that photosynthesis has been taking place.

Where does photosynthesis occur? In the chloroplastids.

Let us now journey into the green cell to see if we can find exactly in what part photosynthesis occurs. Looking through a powerful microscope, we see that the green pigment is not uniformly scattered about the cell, but restricted to small bodies within the cell. These are called chloroplastids. Within the cell of the leaf of *Elodea canadensis,* a common aquarium plant, the chloroplastids can be seen moving in the cell fluid as it streams about the cell. Is it in these chloroplastids where photosynthesis occurs? Yes, apparently so.

Our search is over. Our problems are solved, and we can retire from our investigations with honor and satisfaction. Or can we?

An "energy sink," or storage battery, makes possible the first part of the photosynthetic process.

Scientists have long puzzled over a problem in energetics. The physicist says that light travels in little packages called photons. The quantum energy of each photon depends on its wavelength; the shorter the wavelength the greater the energy. When a chlorophyll molecule absorbs a quantum of blue or red light, the molecule is acti-

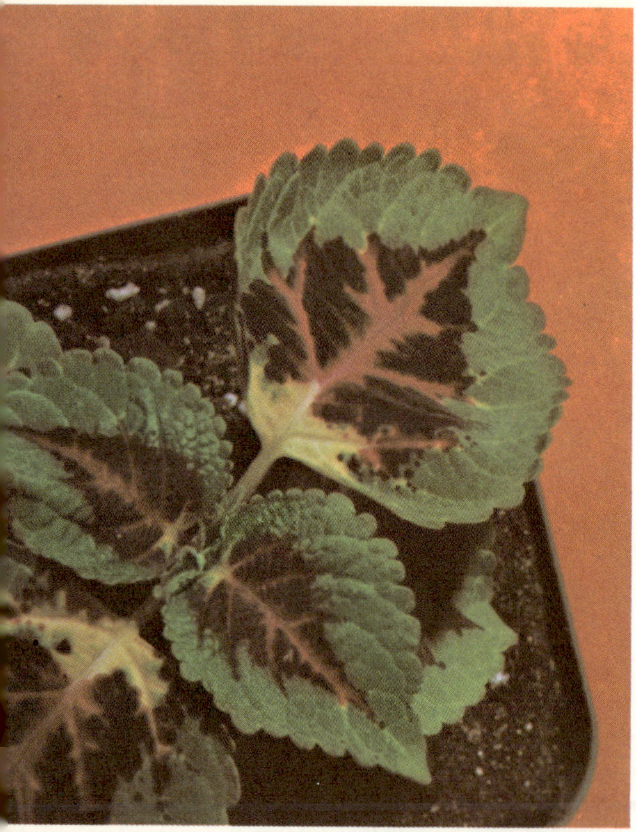
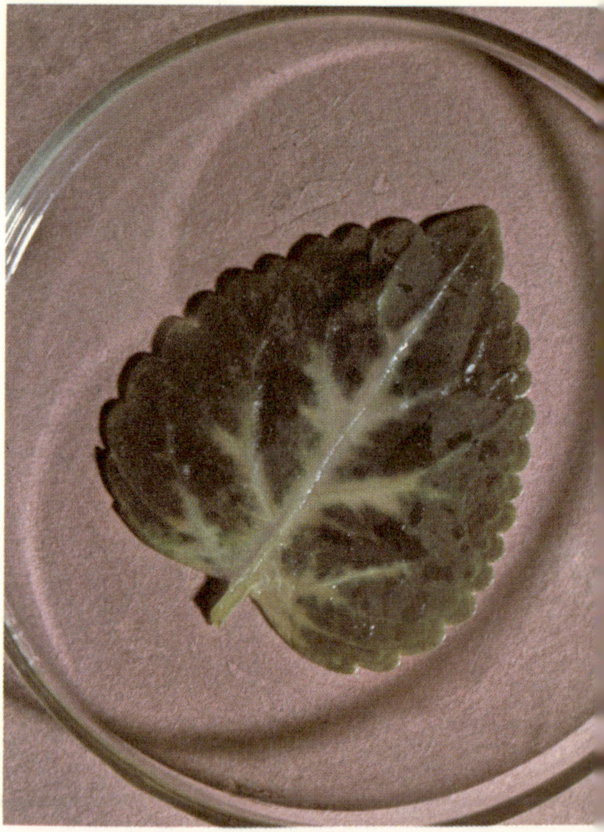
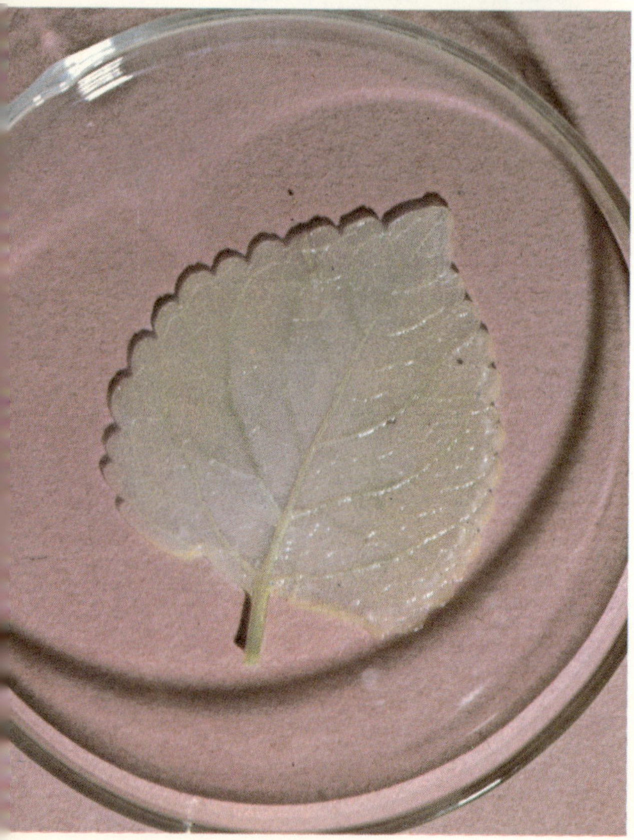
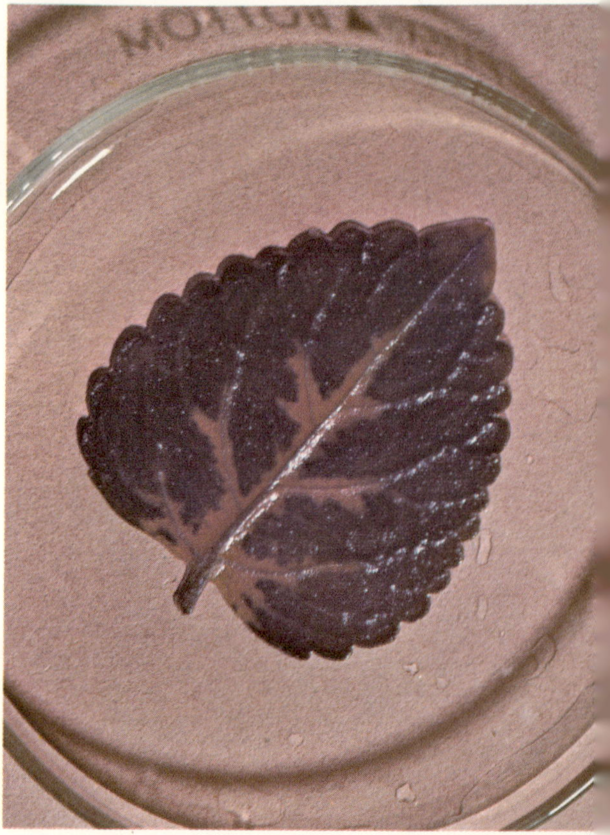

A simple experiment with the Coleus plant (upper left) demonstrates that chlorophyll is involved in photosynthesis. Boiling the leaf in water removes a pigment, leaving (upper right) only the green and white. Boiling in alcohol removes the green chlorophyll, leaving the leaf white (lower left). Iodine solution turns the leaf blue, (lower right) showing the presence of starch, formed by the action of the chlorophyll.

Leaves from the Sierra maple (above, right), starting to change color in the early fall, typify the beauty of green plants and the wonders of chlorophyll and sunlight.

vated. Then what happens? Does this cause photosynthesis to take place, forming sugar and releasing oxygen? No, it isn't that simple. The energy needed to split a molecule of water is about eight times greater than what a quantum of red or blue light has to offer. In the case of our activated chlorophyll molecule there is another problem—time. An activated molecule that cannot use its excess energy gainfully will, in a fraction of a second, give up its energy in the form of useless heat.

Imagine eight men needed to push a car out of a snowdrift. Because of temperament, each individual insists on pushing only when he gets the urge. He gets the

Eight men are needed to push a car out of a snowdrift. But none of the men will push unless he gets the urge, and he feels the urge only once in ten minutes. Will they ever move the car?

urge on an average of once every ten minutes, and the urge lasts about ten seconds. If the men are unwilling or unable to sacrifice their individuality to make a concerted effort, will they ever move the car? No, not unless a machine could be devised that would store up each man's effort until there is enough energy to move the car.

Does chlorophyll have any way of storing up energy from eight quanta of light until it has enough for photosynthesis? Yes, it does! Looking through a high-powered microscope, we can see the way chloroplastids are built. We see small, dense granules called grana scattered about within a less dense matrix called the stroma. In a surface view the grana resemble piles of coins, while a side view shows the lamellar, or platelike, structure of both the grana and the intergrana. Each lamella consists of a layer of protein and a layer of chlorophyll with a fatty layer sandwiched in between. We know from this that chlorophyll molecules are not arranged just any old way within the chloroplast, but in perfect order. Perhaps here we shall discover the "energy sink," or storage battery, so necessary to the first part of the photosynthetic process —the splitting of the water molecule.

In 1957 a scientist by the name of

To make matters worse, the men belong to two rival unions. Hopes to move the car would be slim indeed. Yet, something like this is accomplished within plant cells continually.

Emerson demonstrated to everyone's surprise that two single-color rays of energy, focused together on a single plant, resulted in more photosynthesis than the sum of the photosynthesis when each wavelength acted alone. This gain is known as the "Emerson effect" and is now considered evidence of a "two sink" energy system.

Let's return to our automobile caught in the snowdrift and the eight temperamental men who will not work together to push it out. If we had a "two sink" system here, it would be like dividing our men into two independent labor unions. Now we would need not only a means of pooling the efforts of each individual within each group, but also some liaison between the two groups. Hopes of extricating the car with such a temperamental crew would be slim indeed. Yet, something like this is accomplished within the tiny cells of every green plant constantly, thanks to the marvels of photosynthesis and the complex "energy sinks" upon which it depends. As a result, sugar and starch are manufactured, and we have food to eat.

The quantasome. Could this be the the machine that pries apart the atoms that constitute water?

A recent electron micrograph made by scientists Park and Biggins of the University of California shows a surface view of a granum lamella. Magnified 175,000 times, it shows the lamella itself to be made up of subunits called quantasomes. Each quantasome is large enough to contain between 200 and 300 chlorophyll molecules. Could the quantasome be the long-sought-for machine, the "energy sink," that accumulates the tiny random bursts until, with one mighty thrust, they pry apart the atoms of hydrogen and oxygen constituting the water molecules? It could well be. The oxygen atoms, forsaken by their hydrogen partners, team up two by two to form oxygen molecules. This is the oxygen liberated by photosynthesis—a reaction of sufficient magnitude to renew all the oxygen in the atmosphere once every two thousand years.

Each step of the long trail has revealed orderliness in design and function.

Consider for a moment where man's restless search for understanding of photosynthesis has led. And notice how, at each bend in the long trail, man's mind has been forced to recognize orderliness in design and function.

First there is the sun itself, upon which all life on earth depends, pouring forth streams of light and heat.

Then there is the plant, made of carbon dioxide taken from the air, plus hydrogen atoms from water and chemical elements from the earth.

In the plant leaf is the green cell, with its chlorophyll molecule, which absorbs photons of light, principally blue and red.

Since a single quantum is not strong enough to split a water molecule, the energy is stored in a tiny storage battery until seven other quanta join it.

With the hydrogens released from water and carbon dioxide gas from the atmosphere, the plant makes a molecule of sugar.

Thus we have the creation of food, upon which all plant and animal life depends.

The complexity of photosynthesis confronts us with overwhelming evidence that in our study of plant life we are but following in the steps of the Infinite God.

COURTESY CCM: GENERAL BIOLOGICAL, INC.: CHICAGO

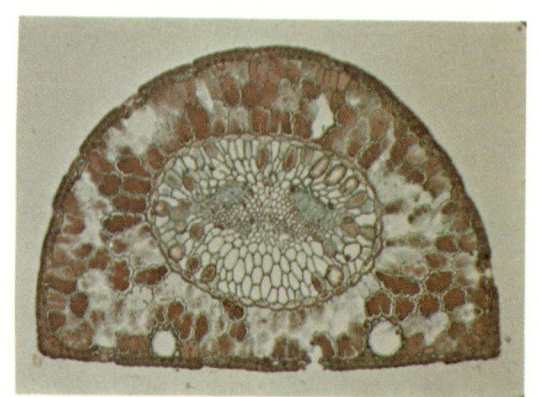

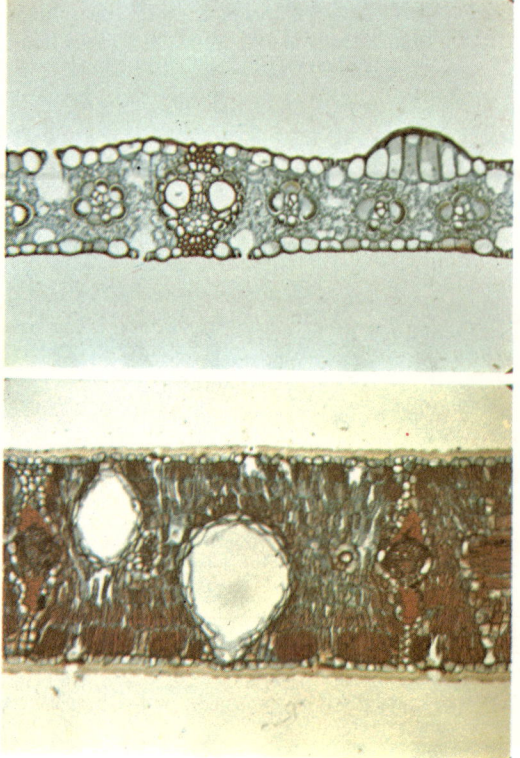

Chlorophyll is basic to trees, shrubs, and all other green plant life.
Large picture: Silver Lake, in the Sierra.
Top, left: cross section of a pine needle.
Middle: corn leaf, cross section.
Bottom: cross section of a leaf from a eucalyptus tree.

46

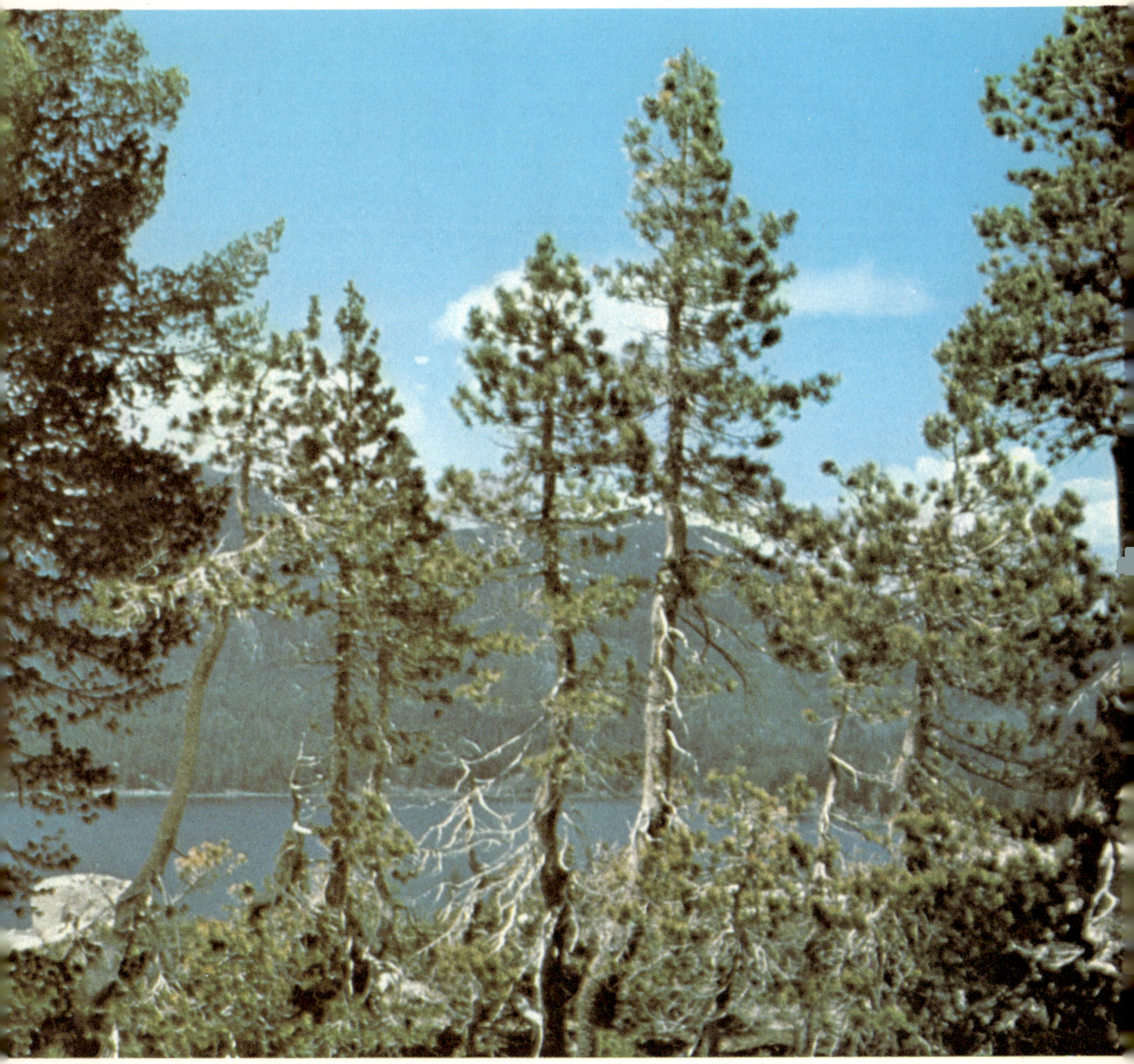

The energy of the universe was "wound up" at the beginning. That all this happened there is no doubt. But how did it happen?

4. The Heart of the Problem

Robert E. D. Clark

Of all the laws of nature, perhaps the most fundamental is concerned with nature's time sense. When events take place, they do so in a way which serves to distinguish between *backwards* and *forwards*. This fact was known to the ancients who made lists of events which never took place in reverse. Rivers did not run uphill, plants and men did not grow backwards, fires did not turn ashes into fully grown trees. At the beginning of the scientific era Newton extended the same idea—warm water never turns back into the hot and cold water from which it is obtained by mixing. Heat, therefore, is becoming degraded and becoming less available.

In the nineteenth century the principle was enshrined in the law of entropy (second law of thermodynamics) and was applied in the theory of the steam engine. Since that time the entropy law, expressed mathematically (it was Boltzmann who showed how this might be done), has been applied in new directions—to the theory of alloys in metallurgy and to communication theory, to give but two examples.

In all instances the basic principle is the same. Events occur in such a way that order disappears, or at best remains unchanged. Entropy, that is to say disorder as applied to the heat motion of molecules, increases. If we think in wider terms, we may say that the *law* of morpholysis (*luo*, I loose, *morphe*, form) is universal, that it has been called "time's arrow."

We are concerned here with a principle fundamental to human

Reprinted by permission from **Christianity Today**, copyright 1959.

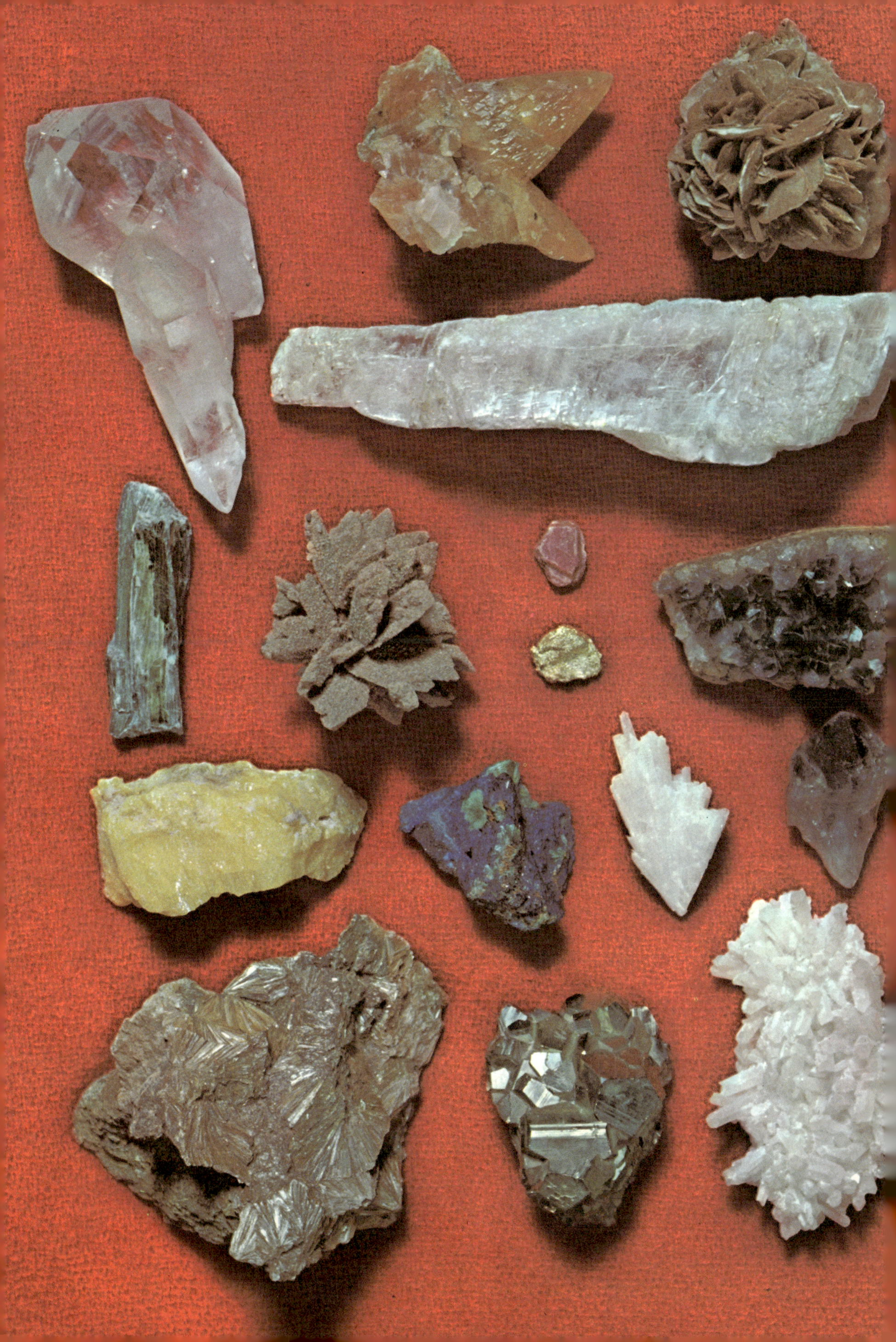

> *In the world of reality, the world of science, events go in one direction only.*

thought. Only in the world of magic or dreams can we fancy a different, a backward trend of events; a world in which a banana, already eaten, emerges whole, or the Niagara Falls is in reverse, an atomic bomb explodes and turns gigantic piles of rubble into houses, streets, and teeming crowds. In the world of reality, the world of science, events go in one direction only. It is a direction in which disorder increases, order is destroyed.

All the laws of nature which are concerned with how things happen are restatements, in a limited field, of the law of morpholysis. So fundamental is this fact to science that we only bother to look for explanations when there seems to be a reversal of this principle. And this explanation which scientists seek to give follows the same pattern. Consider two examples.

A crystal forms in a liquid. Why do the molecules arrange themselves in a beautifully ordered pattern? There are two answers. Firstly, the pattern is not ultimately new, but is a reflection, on a larger scale, of the shapes and other properties of the invisible atoms. This explains why one pattern is chosen by the developing crystal rather than another. Nevertheless, order increases in quantity as the crystal forms. This is compensated for by a corresponding loss of order in the fluid from which the crystals separated—it is left hotter than before: its molecules are in greater confusion.

Again how is biological reproduction possible? The answer is basically the same. The form of the plant or animal is a reflection of the shapes and properties of the genes. And as the plant or animal reaches maturity, the increase in the *amount* of its organization (but not the type of organization—why this corresponds, say, to a sheep rather than a buttercup) is compensated for by loss in the order of its surroundings: energy stored in food or in sunlight is degraded.

The energy of our universe was "wound up" at the beginning; the elements came into existence endowed with their potentialities.

The answers we have given in these two examples are typical of the answers which science must give to every problem that is posed. Only when an answer can be given along these lines is it even possible to *begin* to tackle the thousand and one questions of detail which must arise if a full understanding is to be reached. *If we cannot start to answer a question at this level, then we may just as well invoke magic. We are demanding that an explanation should be sought in terms which are inconsistent with scientific thought.*

Now the startling point emerges that whenever we look into the question of origins we find that, at some stages at least,

A crystal's pattern is a reflection, on a larger scale, of the properties of the invisible atoms. (1 and 16) Quartz; (2) calcite; (3 and 6) gypsum; (4) selenite; (5) serpentine; (7) ruby; (8) crystalline gold; (9 and 13) amethyst; (14) pyrophyllite; (15) pyrites.

events *must* have taken place to which answers of the kind considered cannot be given.

The energy of the universe was "wound up" at the beginning; in all subsequent events it has become less and less available. The chemical elements came into existence endowed from the start with astonishingly "ordered" potentialities. Was it chance that gave hydrogen, carbon, nitrogen, oxygen, and the rest their remarkable properties, many of which are so fundamental to life? Our planet also came to be placed at the right distance from the sun, with oceans to keep its temperature even, with tilted axis to give the seasons, with its weight correct to allow of the escape of hydrogen but the retention of oxygen, and so on.

Somehow life came, and we are part of the story. But how did it happen?

And somehow or other life came: three-dimensional structures of atoms, arranged in shapes of bewildering complexity, blue-printed with instructions for self-reproduction! With the passing of time new and yet more intricate structures came into being: elaborate mechanisms for flight; equipment for detecting position relative to surroundings by picking up reflected electromagnetic rays; fantastic gadgets for effecting orientation in gravitational fields; pumps, complete with valves and elaborate timing mechanisms, for pumping fluids; mechanisms for detecting and relaying information about touch, heat, cold, and injury; mechanisms for picking up and interpreting rhythmic atmospheric disturbances at fantastically low energy levels and yet capable of responding without injury to levels a thousand billion times as great; objects like gigantic telephone exchanges connected with subscribers by the *billion*— And so we might continue indefinitely, for new mechanisms are continually coming to light.

That all this happened there is no doubt. We ourselves are part of the story. But how did it happen? Can we even begin to answer the question along the lines that we employ when we commence to tackle every

These three things, if they

A nuclear explosion can turn a teeming city into a vast heap of rubble

Hot and cold water combine to make warm water, as we would expect.

Likewise, theories of evolution postulate magic—the creation, spon-

could happen, would be a backward trend, a reversal of nature and science.

in an instant. But the reverse of this could never occur. Only in the world of fancy, imagination, or magic do such things happen in reverse.

But warm water poured out will never separate itself into hot and cold. This "event" goes in one direction only, with disorder increasing.

taneously, mysteriously, in complete absence of observers, of radically new types of organization: the reversal of the law of morpholysis.

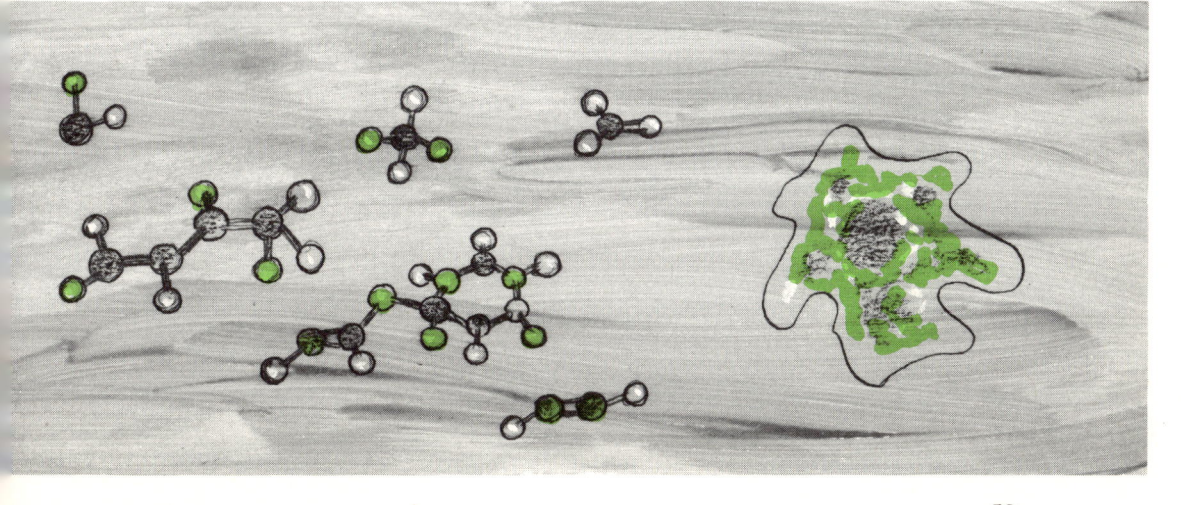

other problem that science poses? It seems not. We can understand how a new type of order, once established, can multiply by degrading chemical compounds and quanta of light, but how do thousands of new kinds of order arise?

As well might one expect an enormous sale of wheelless automobiles, hoping they might prove useful as rabbit hutches.

A century ago Darwin suggested that chance variations, followed by the survival of the fittest, would, in the end, give rise to the appearance of design. Perhaps he was right—within the limits of the very simple. Yet few suppose that Darwin's theory goes to the heart of the problem.

Survival of the fittest could not explain the ordered nature of the energy of the universe, nor the properties of the chemical elements, nor the origin of the first forms of life which must have possessed great complexity in order to be alive at all. And although the idea has been a commonplace for a century, it has as yet done nothing to solve major biological difficulties, though it has done a good deal to solve minor ones.

Biological structures, like all functional structures, must be all there at once or they serve no purpose. A car without its wheels or a tape recorder without its tape will, in terms of natural selection, be rejected as useless. Yet highly specialized organs are found in nature; and it is hard, indeed, to suppose that they could all have arisen gradually. In some cases suggestions have been made as to the uses which uncompleted structures might have had. But common sense revolts against the suggestion that all cases can be explained along these lines. As well might one expect an enormous sale of wheelless automobiles on the ground that, by an off chance, they would prove useful as rabbit hutches.

Even more basic is the difficulty afforded by size. It is a principle in engineering that one cannot, simply, imitate a small machine on a much larger scale. There comes a time when mere modification will not do; a basic redesign is called for. This fact arises from the consideration that weight increases as the cube of dimensions, but surface area and forces, which can be transmitted by wires, tendons, or muscles, vary only as the square. For this reason a fly the size of a dog would break its legs and a dog the size of a fly would be unable to maintain its body heat. So if evolution started with very small organisms there would come a time when, as a result of size increase, small naturally selected modifications would no longer prove useful. Radically new designs would be necessary for survival. But by its very nature, natural selection could not provide for such redesign.

It would be easier to show by science that evolution is impossible than to explain how it happened.

From all this and much more besides, it becomes increasingly clear that it would be easier to show by science that evolution is impossible than to explain how it happened. The difficulties are, in fact, so great that we may well wonder why they are not more often recognized. But perhaps they are. In the nineteenth century scientists hoped to discover *truth* about nature. Today, many say that not truth but the creation of theories which will stimulate discovery and thought is the aim of science. Darwin's theory of evolution is certainly of this kind. So the biologist will sometimes say, quite blandly, that for him it is a choice between something he does not really believe in or nothing at all. "No amount of

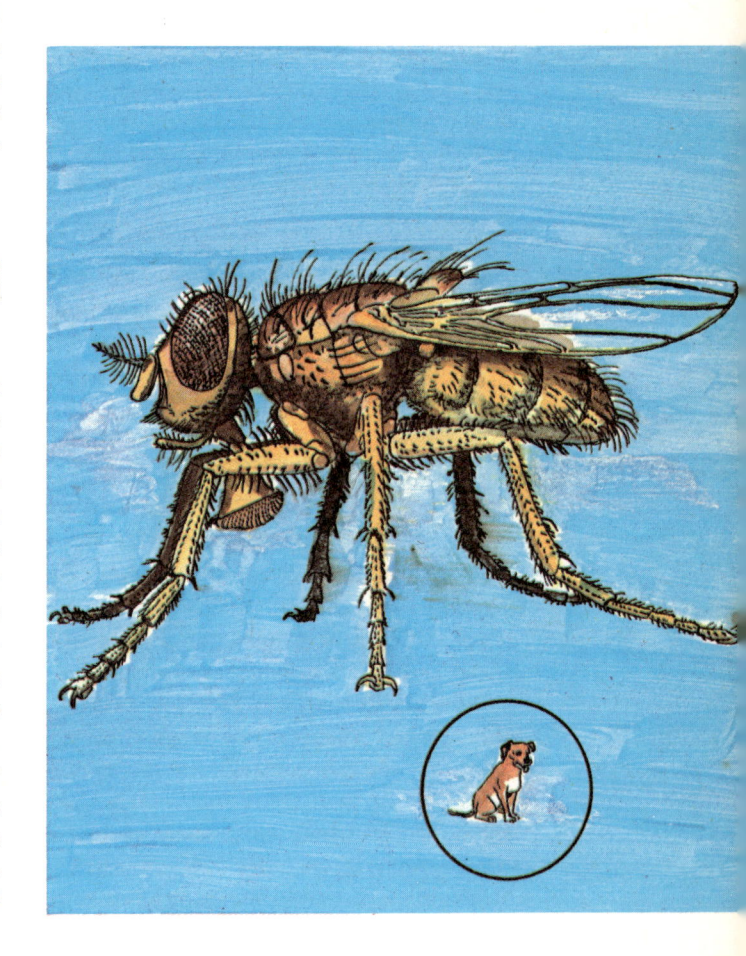

A fly the size of a dog would break its legs, and a fly-sized dog could not maintain its body heat. If evolution started with small organisms, the time would come when radically new designs would be necessary for survival. But by its very nature, natural selection could not provide for such redesign.

argument or clever epigram, can disguise the inherent improbability of orthodoxy [orthodox evolutionary theory]," writes Professor Gray of Cambridge (England), "but most biologists think that it is better to think in terms of improbable events than not to think at all."—*Nature*, 1954, pages 173, 227.

If we say God made the world, are we not resorting to magic? Creation by the use of the mind, by creative effort, is not magic.

Facing the evidence fairly, it is clear that no matter where we look we find confirmation of the Biblical doctrine that "the things which are seen were not made of things which do appear." But if we say that God created the world, or life, or did this or that, are we not resorting to explanations of the magical kind? Are we not turning our backs on science?

There are two answers to this. First, it is easy to postulate magic without realizing the fact. This is, in effect, just what theories of evolution do. While paying lip service to science, they postulate something opposed to the basic principle of all scientific thought—they postulate the creation, spontaneously, magically, in complete absence of observers, of radically new types of organization: the actual reversal of the law of morpholysis! If, then, when we say that God created the world, we are resorting to magic as an explanation, we do no worse than the materialistic evolutionist. Indeed, our attitude is to be preferred to his, for we do not disguise magic behind high-sounding words which are intended to sound scientific.

But, secondly, we must not forget that there is within the experience of each of us a nonmagical principle which is able to reverse the law of morpholysis. By thinking, by putting forth creative effort, we can create the very order that may so easily and so spontaneously be destroyed. Now this principle of creativity in the mind of man is *not* magic. Magic works without effort. You mutter "abracadabra," and the thing is done. But the man who spends years writing a book or designing a bridge knows that "power is gone out of him." He creates by faith and by effort, not by magic.

When we think of the ultimate origins of nature, we see many evidences of plan—or what looks like plan. It is as if the major (though not all the minor) instances of organization are the product of a Mind, of a kind not unlike our own, though unimaginably greater and more competent. It seems natural and sensible to take the evidence at its face value; to believe that God created the heaven and the earth. But there is no need to think of God as an almighty magician. The Bible speaks often of the forethought and care which God put into the creation (we even read that He rested from His labors), and in science we see vindication of its teaching. We ourselves, made in the image of God, are not magicians, and there is no need to think of God as a magician either.

> Within the experience of each of us is a nonmagical principle which can reverse the law of morpholysis. By thinking, by creative effort, we can produce order and design. Thus, when we think of origins in nature, we see evidences of a Mind, not unlike our own, though unimaginably greater and more competent. It is sensible to take the evidence at face value; to believe that God created the heaven and the earth. What sensitive attention to beauty, for instance, entered into the design of the snow plant which springs from the forest floor as snowbanks recede in the spring!

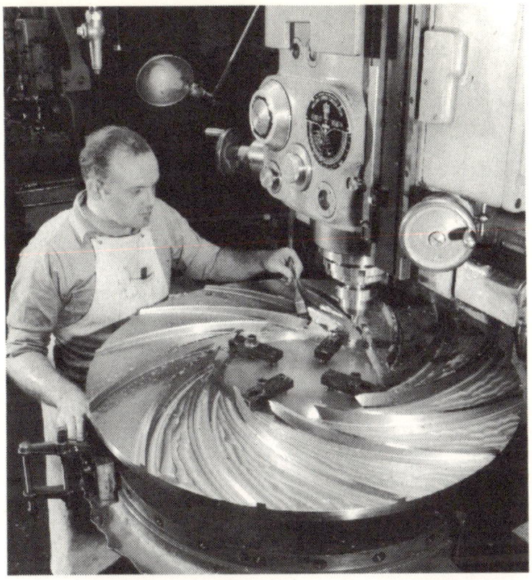
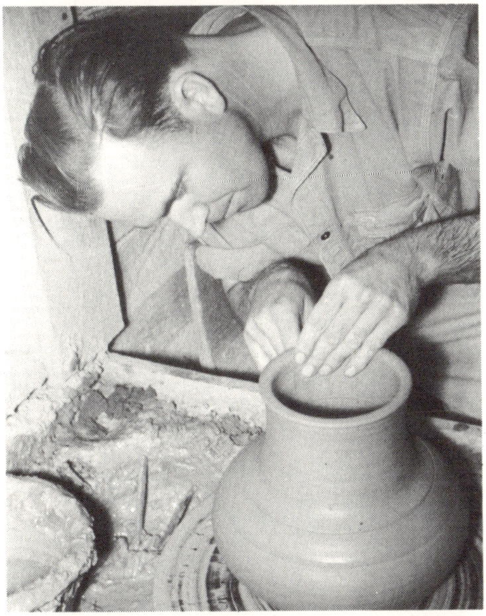
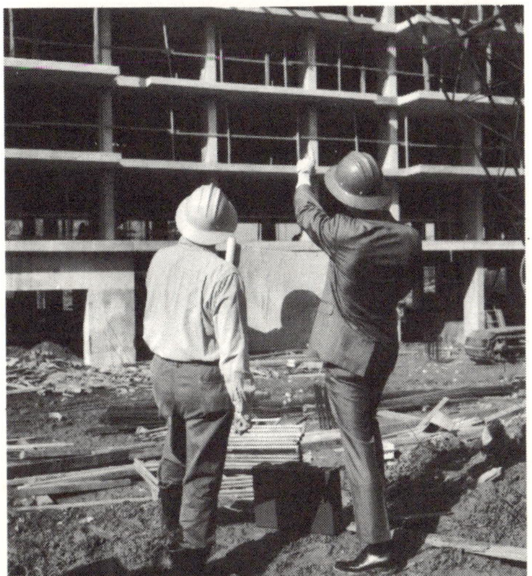
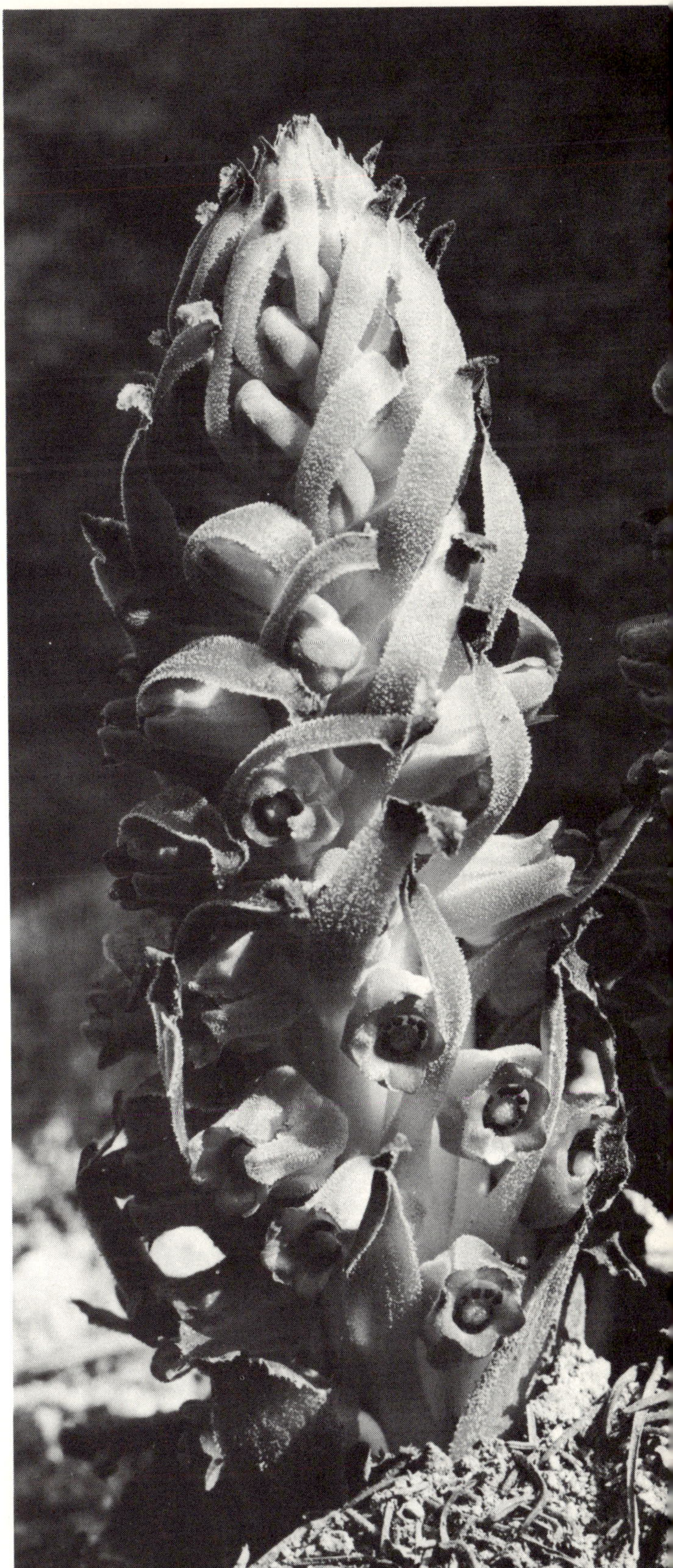

TRILOBITE
(Five times actual size)

5.
Fossils From the Ancient Seas

Harold G. Coffin

Scientist Charles Walcott was exploring high in the Canadian Rockies when he found a piece of ancient ocean floor. What had been mud long before had hardened into a type of rock scientists call "Middle Cambrian shale" and had been lifted several thousand feet above sea level, to become the side of a mountain. This particular shale, Walcott noticed, contained fossil sea creatures.

His discovery, made in 1910, turned out to be one of the most complete collections of Cambrian fossil creatures known. Here were sea worms, jellyfish, crustaceans, and trilobites. Many of the specimens were soft-bodied animals that left detailed impressions in the fine-grained shale. An amazing array of segmented worms was discovered; and the impressions, looking almost like X-ray pictures, still showed the details of spines, bristles, and hairs. Even the digestive organs and other soft parts of some could be seen. In some of the shrimp-like creatures the detail was complete down to the small appendages and mouth parts.

One of the most striking of the fossils was the trilobite. This extinct animal somewhat resembled the sow bug, or pill bug, that we sometimes find under stones and flowerpots. The sow bug can roll up into a tight ball about the size of a pea. Trilobites also could roll up into balls, and sometimes their fossil remains are found that way in the ground. Along with insects, crustaceans, spiders, and a few other creeping things, trilobites belong to the Arthropoda, or joint-legged creatures. Some fossil trilobites are over a foot long, but most specimens measure less than six inches.

When living, the trilobites all looked basically similar, but some were eyeless while others had huge compound eyes. Long spines extended from the corners of the head, body, or tail of some species, but others were smooth all the way around. Most species crawled on the bottom of the ocean, but a few were burrowing creatures, and some may have been good swimmers.

The Peripatus—a connecting link in the evolution of segmented worms to insects?

Another unusual fossil found in the shale was a caterpillar-like worm related to the living *Peripatus*. It had stubby appendages not jointed like the legs of insects. A true caterpillar is one form in the life cycle of an insect, but this worm maintained its larval appearance throughout its adult life. *Peripatus* has been considered an intermediate stage in the evolution of segmented worms to insects. But, if this worm is such a connecting link, this evolutionary step had already been taken by the time this Cambrian ocean bed formed. So scientists have spent much time searching the lower, older strata (Precambrian strata) for evidences of earlier creatures, ancestors to these whose remains have been found. What have been the results?

Walcott himself thought he had discovered many species of fossil algae in the Precambrian, but later students have rejected most of these. More recently (1961), discovery of some Precambrian fossils was reported in Australia, but further examination showed that the fossils probably were Cambrian. Precambrian worm burrows have been reported from the Grand Canyon; and these, together with a few filaments of pond scums, molds, and algae are the only reasonably certain examples of Precambrian fossils. Despite a great deal of searching in sediments below the Cambrian, little has been discovered.

Where did these creatures come from? —a perplexing question.

Where, then, did this oceanful of creatures come from, if the layer below them does not reveal their ancestors? Why did

Well-preserved fossil trilobites occur abundantly in the Burgess Shale of the Middle Cambrian. Here Dr. and Mrs. Charles Walcott direct collecting from a rich deposit on Mount Stephen in British Columbia.

these worms, mollusks, lamp shells, trilobites, sponges, jellyfish, and the rest appear so suddenly? Evolutionists have been wondering, and some are frankly perplexed.

Even Charles Darwin realized this was a crucial point, and wrote in *Origin of Species:* "To the question why we do not find rich fossiliferous deposits belonging to these assumed earliest periods prior to the Cambrian system, I can give no satisfactory answer.... The case at present must remain inexplicable; and may be truly urged as a valid argument against the views here entertained."

A century of intensive search for fossils in the Precambrian rocks has thrown little light on the problem.

In Darwin's day few people had studied fossils. They could argue, "Wait; this apparent lack of fossils in the Precambrian rocks, and the sudden appearance of many kinds in the Cambrian, is due to insufficient collecting. Give us time to do more searching."

Exactly 100 years later, Dr. Norman D. Newell of Columbia University, in reading a paper prepared for the Darwin centennial celebrations, said, "A century of intensive search for fossils in the Precambrian rocks has thrown very little light on this problem. Early theories that those rocks were dominantly nonmarine or that once-contained fossils have been destroyed by heat and pressure have been abandoned because the Precambrian rocks of many districts physically are very similar to younger rocks in all respects except that they rarely contain any records whatsoever of past life."[1]

A number of theories have been advanced to attempt to explain this situation. Briefly, as summarized by Dr. D. I. Axelrod of the University of California, they are as follows: (1) Precambrian animals had no skeletons because they contained no calcium. (2) Precambrian seas were acid, and this prevented the development of calcium skeletons. (3) The strata are composed of land deposits which are not ideal for the preservation of fossils. (4) Life originated in fresh water and migrated down rivers to the seas by Cambrian times. (5) Precambrian organisms were not bottom dwellers, so did not require hard parts —shells or skeletons. (6) The adoption of an attached mode of life made necessary the development of skeletal parts during the Cambrian. (7) Precambrian organisms lived along the seashores where erosion was likely to obliterate the organic remains. (8) Gross mutations occurred to living organisms at the beginning of the Cambrian, which increased their complexity, variety, and size. (9) Precambrian specimens are too small to be seen readily by usual collecting methods. (10) The Cambrian represents a lot of time, and life has not arisen as quickly as it may appear.

None of these ten suggested solutions is adequate; the mystery remains unsolved.

That none of these are really very adequate solutions is evident to the thoughtful student.

Dr. Axelrod gives a good statement of the situation: "One of the major unsolved problems of geology and evolution is the occurrence of diversified, multicellular marine invertebrates in Lower Cambrian rocks on all the continents and their absence in rocks of greater age. These Early Cambrian fossils include porifera, coelenterates, brachiopods, mollusca, echinoids, and arthropods. In the Arthropoda are included the well-known trilobites, which are complexly organized, with well-differentiated head and tail, numerous thoracic parts, jointed legs and—like the later crustaceans—a complex respiratory system. . . . Their high degree of organization clearly indicates that a long period of evolution preceded their appearance in the record. However, when we turn to examine the Precambrian rocks for the forerunners of these Early Cambrian fossils, they are nowhere to be found. Many thick (over 5,000 feet) sections of sedimentary rock are now known to lie in unbroken succession below strata containing the earliest Cambrian fossils. These sediments apparently were suitable for the preservation of fossils because they often are found in them. Clearly, a significant but unrecorded chapter in the history of life is missing from the rocks of Precambrian time."[2]

The intermediate steps or missing links are still missing along the chain of living things.

Dr. G. G. Simpson of Harvard University, one of the foremost authorities on prehistoric life, says that the sudden appearance of life is "not only the most puzzling feature of the whole fossil record but also its greatest apparent inadequacy."[3]

Another puzzler for the evolutionist is the fact that the ancient Cambrian sea creatures can be classified as basically the same as sea creatures living today. This is the problem of the "missing links." The intermediate steps or missing links are still missing all along the chain of living things. During the hundred years since Charles Darwin's book was published, only a very few fossils have been found that occupy a position between the basic kinds of animals, and even these are subject to debate. Dr. Newell says: "These isolated discoveries, of course, stimulate hope that more complete records will be found and other gaps closed. These finds are, however, rare; and experience shows that the gaps which separate the highest categories may never be bridged in the fossil record. Many of the discontinuities tend to be more and more emphasized with increased collecting."[4]

Dr. G. G. Simpson, writing in a volume commemorating the appearance of Charles Darwin's *Origin of Species,* clearly states the case: "It is a feature of the known fossil record that most taxa [kinds of animals and plants] appear abruptly. They are not as a rule led up to by a sequence of almost imperceptibly changing forerunners such as Darwin believed should be usual in evolution. . . . When a new genus appears in the record it is usually well separated morphologically from the most nearly similar other known genera. This phenomenon becomes more universal and more intense as the hierarchy of categories is ascended."[5]

Both of these problems, the appearance of fossils in the Cambrian with no traceable ancestors and the persistent gaps between major kinds of organisms, are extremely important to evolution. If either or both of these problems cannot be solved (and they have not been solved for over a hun-

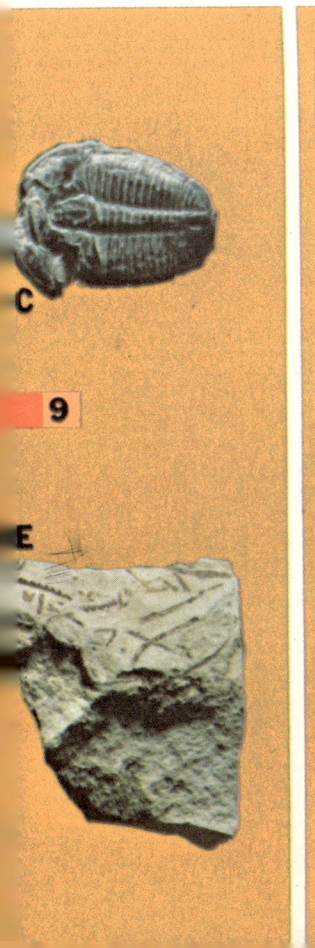

Seven Cambrian fossils: A, B, C, and F are varieties of trilobites from Utah and California. D is a specimen of fossil algae from Saratoga Springs, New York. E is a graptolite from Minnesota, and G, a brachiopod from Utah. The apparently sudden appearance of life is "the most puzzling feature of the fossil record" and "its greatest . . . inadequacy."

dred years), the theory of progressive evolution must be considered unproved. At best, it is based not on fact only, but on faith also. Dr. Simpson, although convinced that progressive evolution has occurred, admits that "these peculiarities of the record pose one of the most important theoretical problems in the whole history of life."[6]

Is it not time to admit that much of the evidence for progressive evolution is lacking in its most essential features, and to find an explanation that fits the evidence?

One cannot help wondering what Charles Darwin would do if he were alive today. Would he concede on the basis of his own statement in Origin of Species that evolution of major groups has not occurred? One can only speculate about this, but it is hoped that he would not retreat into the thicket of excuses that has been used by many others since his time.

One explanation for the absence of the Cambrian ancestors and intermediate links was not listed in the series of ten explanations given earlier. Faced with the strong evidence, a few scientists have suggested an

64

Creatures that lived in the lower Paleozoic era included (1) branching sponges, (2) crinoids, (3) brachiopods, (4 and 5) mollusks, (6) jellyfish, and (7) trilobites. Where did this oceanful of creatures come from, if the layer below them does not reveal their ancestors?

In Precambrian strata, pond scums, molds, algae, and possible worm burrows are the only reasonably certain examples of fossils. (8) worm burrows, (9) algae.

A proposed reconstruction of the history of the ancient seas.

Can we reconstruct briefly the history of the ancient seas? In the beginning God created the earth and furnished it with water which contained many suitable habitats for living organisms. He created the life and filled the seas with form and variety. At some later time, erosion filled these seas with thousands of feet of sediments. Then pressures within the crust squeezed the sediments; breaking, lifting, and overthrusting them above the adjacent land. Erosion by water, wind, and ice widened and deepened the valleys, gorges, and faults, eventually creating the Rocky Mountains. Nothing resembling the ancient oceans is left except the delicately preserved remains of the animals that lived and died there.

The creatures left no traces of evolutionary ancestors. Was it because they had none?

As we dig into the rocks and look at the fossils buried in these uplifted sediments, we come away convinced that no gradual development from simple to complex has occurred in the history of life on the earth. An intelligent Creator filled the seas with swarms of living creatures of many diverse types. When they died and were buried in the accumulating ocean sediments, they left no traces of evolutionary ancestors because they had none.

explosive type of evolution that quickly populated the ancient seas. This is one step short of saying that a Creator formed them and thus quickly caused the seas to be filled with organisms. This concept is in harmony with the Holy Scriptures and beautifully solves both fundamental problems described above. Is it not time, after these many years, to look the situation squarely in the face and admit that most of the evidence for progressive evolution is lacking in its most essential features? And is it not time to turn to an explanation that more nearly fits the evidence?

REFERENCES

1. Norman D. Newell, "The Nature of the Fossil Record," *Proceedings of the American Philosophical Society*, April 1959, 103(2), pages 264-285.
2. D. I. Axelrod, "Early Cambrian Marine Fauna," *Science*, 1958, 128(3314), pages 7-9.
3. George G. Simpson, "The History of Life," in *The Evolution of Life* (University of Chicago Press, 1960), pages 117-180.
4. Newell, *op. cit.*
5. Simpson, *op. cit.*
6. *Ibid.*

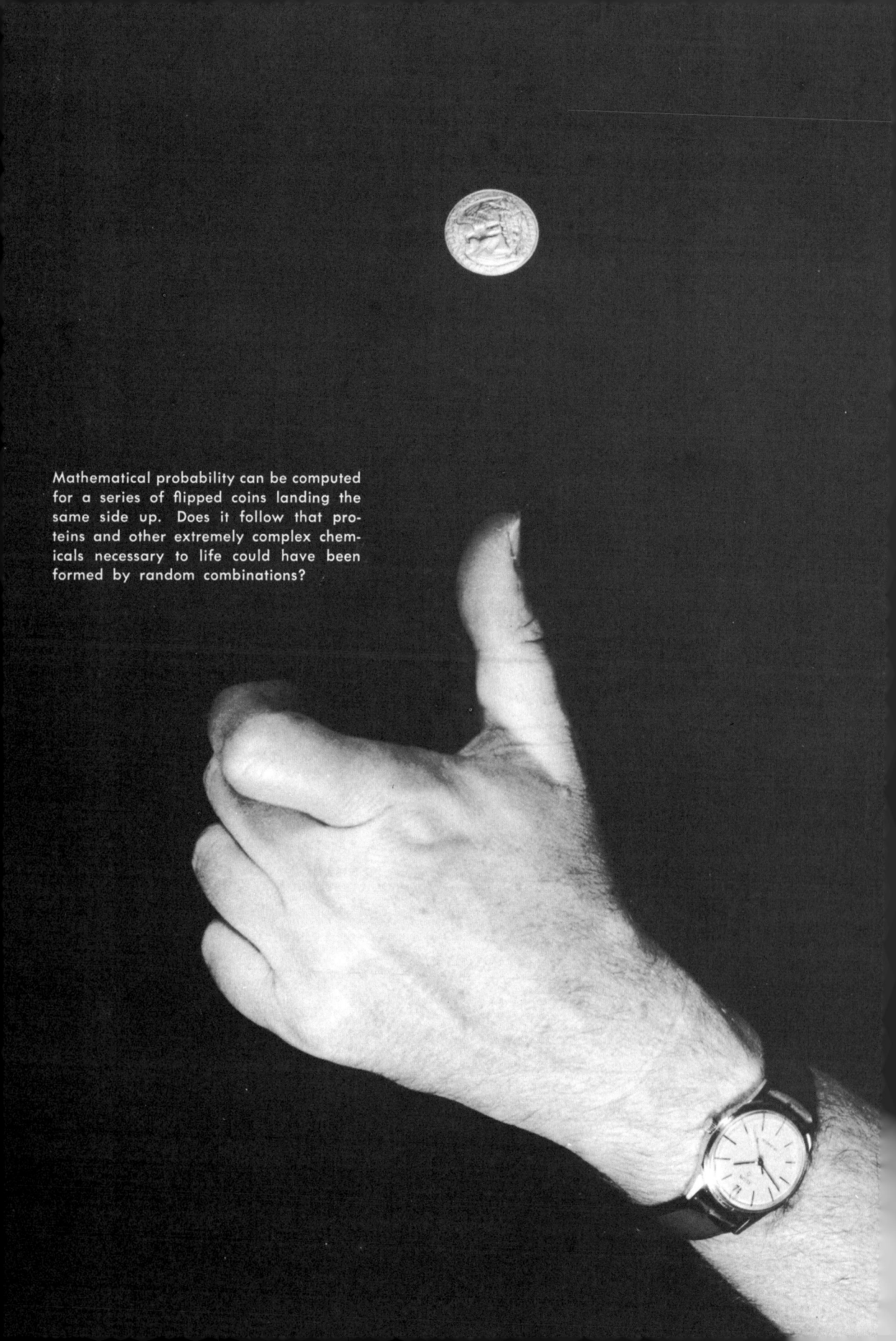

Mathematical probability can be computed for a series of flipped coins landing the same side up. Does it follow that proteins and other extremely complex chemicals necessary to life could have been formed by random combinations?

6.
Proteins and Probability

L. E. Downs

When I took a class in printing some years ago, I spent many hours laboriously setting type by hand, one letter at a time. Then, toward the end of the course, the teacher arranged a field trip to San Francisco, where we visited some large publishing concerns. There for the first time I saw a monotype, which really impressed me. With no operator in the room, this machine, all by itself, was swiftly casting and setting up the type to print a book.

The monotype was invented many years before anyone coined the word "automation," but it works on that principle. It gets instructions from a tape an operator has already punched with holes on another machine. Today sophisticated machines perform vastly more complicated tasks, but they can do nothing at all unless someone supplies a program of coded instructions. And the programs must be developed by intelligent human beings.

Although man-made automated machinery is relatively new, automation itself has been here for a long time. Every living creature is an automatic molecular "machine" operating on a program of instructions vastly more sophisticated than any human invention.

How did these amazingly complex programs originate? By random processes operating over long ages, some say. Is this possible? Before we try to answer the question, let's look into some of the complexities of these living machines. In order to understand them, we must first know something of the chemistry of proteins and nucleic acids.

In living systems proteins function as building materials; most are enzymes—those vital sparks that keep the body "machinery" running. Chemists call them organic catalysts—substances that speed up a chemical reaction while the catalysts themselves remain unchanged. Thus a small amount of enzyme can transform a very large amount of the material it acts upon. For example, if you mix starch with hydrochloric acid, the starch slowly breaks down into two sugars, maltose and glucose, and a substance called dextrin. But in your digestive tract, starch-splitting enzymes do a more complete job, and they do it at high speed.

Within each living cell are quantities of proteins; 53 billion molecules in a single liver cell.

Each enzyme is made to do a specific job. Each one can catalyze only one kind of chemical reaction. A starch-splitting enzyme will have no effect on a protein, and vice versa. In fact, some enzymes can split a protein molecule only at certain sites on the molecule. To be so specific in function, each enzyme or protein must, of course, be unique in the structure of its molecules.

We have mentioned only a few of the familiar digestive enzymes, and they act on foods in the digestive tract. But, inside, each living cell has enormous numbers of enzymes. Within a single bacterial cell (*Escherichia coli*) are an estimated 1,000,000 to 3,000,000 protein molecules, including from 2,000 to 10,000 different *kinds* of enzymes, all in a space 1/25,000 of an inch in diameter and 3/25,000 of an inch long.

A single liver cell contains an estimated 53,000,000,000 protein molecules, which would probably include tens of thousands of different kinds of enzymes, all organized into a smoothly running cellular "machine." No one knows how many kinds of proteins are found in all of the kinds of plants and animals in the world, but there must be many billions. And this is only the beginning!

Introducing the amino acids, the building blocks of proteins.

How can there be so many kinds of proteins, each with its specific job to do? What are proteins made of, anyway? Protein molecules are long chains of amino acid molecules linked together. Since a single protein molecule may be made of several hundred amino acids, and since there are more than twenty different kinds of amino acids, the number of possible kinds of protein is almost infinite. See diagram on the next page.

Two amino acids linked together form a dipeptide. Three make a tripeptide, and longer chains are polypeptides. A protein is one polypeptide or a combination of several with a specific function in a living plant or animal.

The hormone insulin, a protein taken by diabetics, has rather small molecules, each consisting of two polypeptide chains, with a total of fifty-one amino acids. Much more complex is the human hemoglobin molecule, whose protein portion consists of 574 amino acids arranged in four polypeptide chains. There are two α chains with 141 amino acids each and two β chains with 146 amino acids each.

DIAGRAMS OF AMINO ACID MOLECULES

Here (top figure) is a simple way to represent a molecule of an amino acid. Black stands for a carbon atom; blue is nitrogen; red is oxygen; yellow is hydrogen; and brown represents a radical (an atom or group of atoms). ▶

The amino acids found in living tissues differ from each other in the composition of the radical. If the radical is a hydrogen atom, then the amino acid is glycine, pictured opposite. ▶

Serine is more complex, with R (the radical) replaced by a group of atoms. ▶

Two amino acids linked together form a dipeptide. ▶

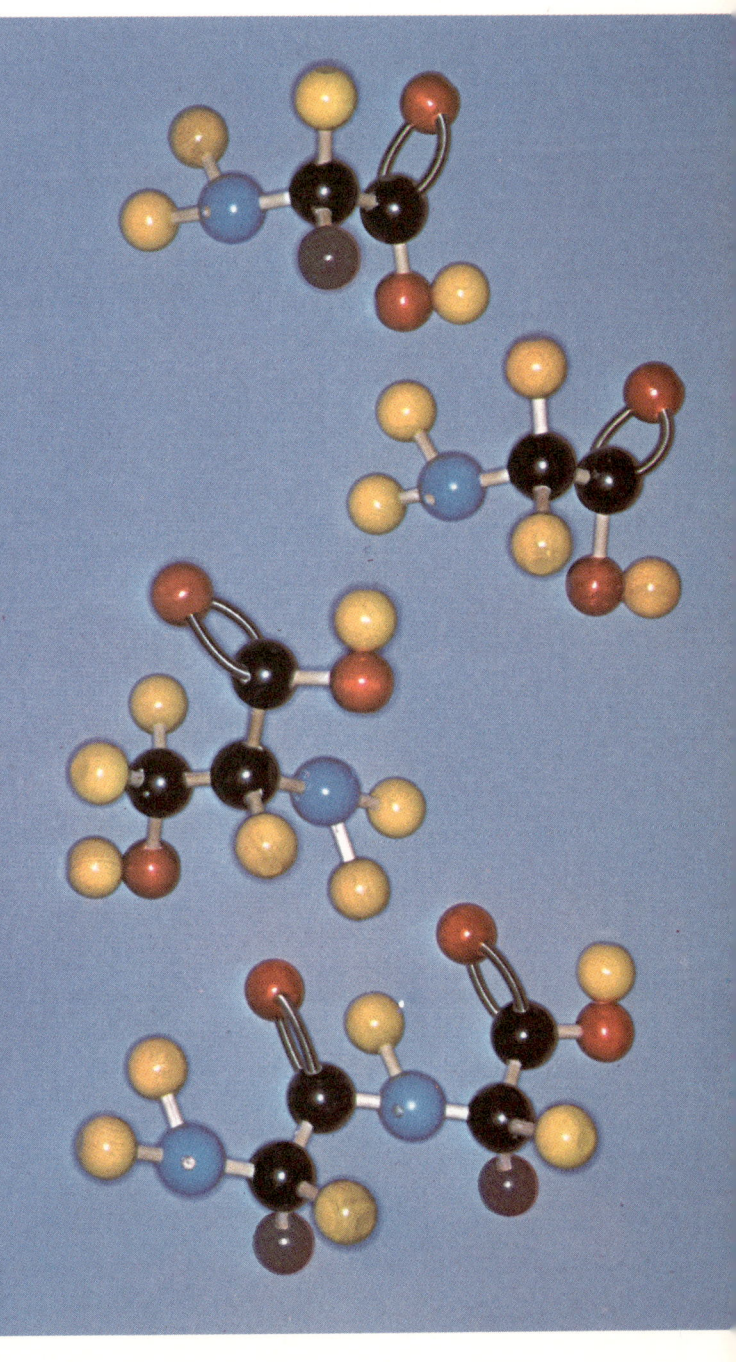

69

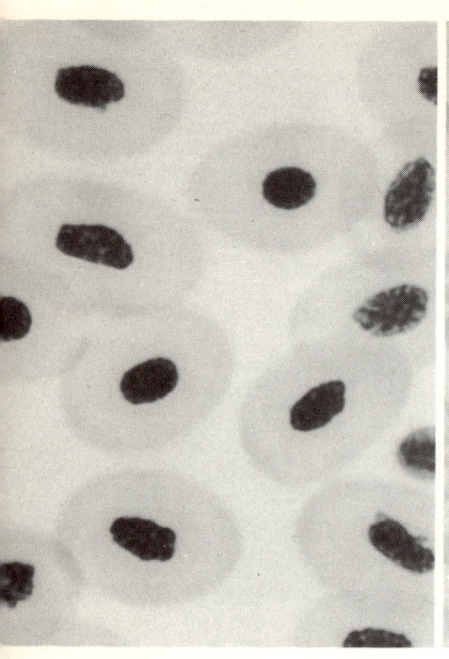

CAT BLOOD 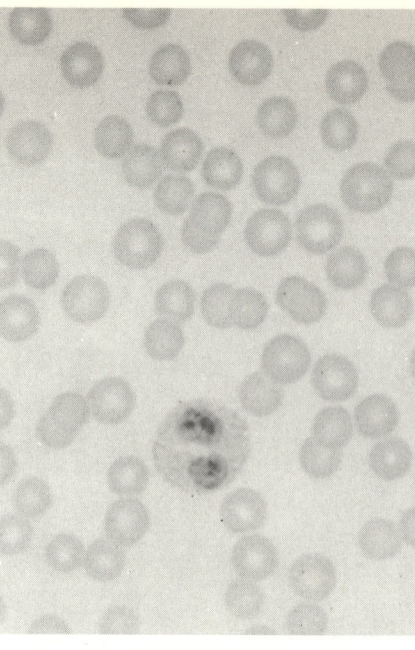   FROG BLOOD 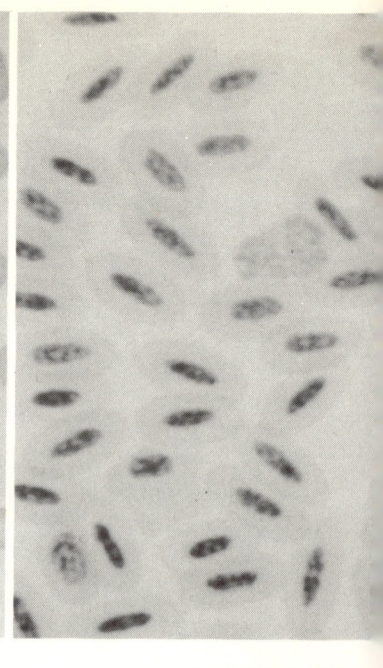   PIGEON BLOOD

To do its specific job, a protein must usually have a precise sequence of amino acids. Most major variations make it impossible for the protein to perform its work. The following sequences are those at the beginning of the β chain of normal human hemoglobin (A), and of two abnormal hemoglobins (S and C):

- Hemoglobin A—valine, histidine, leucine, threonine, proline, glutamic acid, glutamic acid
- Hemoglobin S—valine, histidine, leucine, threonine, proline, valine, glutamic acid
- Hemoglobin C—valine, histidine, leucine, threonine, proline, lysine, glutamic acid

The amino acid sequences of about a dozen abnormal human hemoglobins have been worked out, and in all of them there is a single amino acid substitution. In the case of hemoglobin S, certain substitutions of just *one* out of 146 amino acids would make human life impossible. Some of the other substitutions are not so serious.

A study of the β chains from hemoglobin molecules from fourteen species of vertebrate animals reveals amino acid substitu-

When hemoglobins from blood cells of different species are compared, much variation appears. And the data from human blood suggests that each kind of hemoglobin is precisely tailored to function in the red cells of the species in which it is found.

tions at 54 of the 146 positions. Although a given position usually has a single substitution, sometimes there are two or even three. The amino acid sequences of insulin from cattle, pigs, sheep, horses, and two species of whales also illustrate this. The insulin molecules from these six species are identical except for the amino acids occupying positions eight, nine, and ten of the α chain.

So it is evident that the highly specific nature of the proteins is due to unique, precise sequences of amino acids. In man, all variants from the fixed sequences estab-

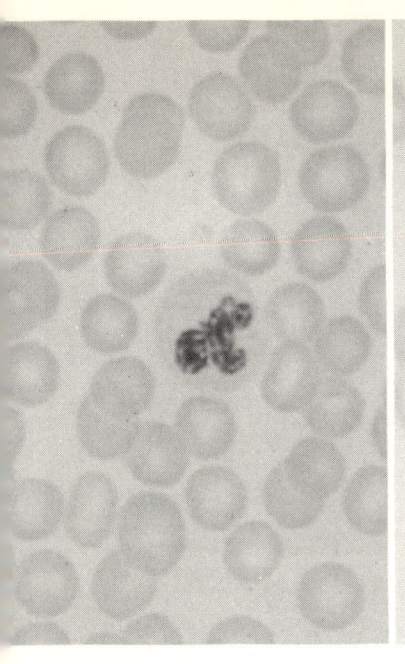

| HUMAN BLOOD | 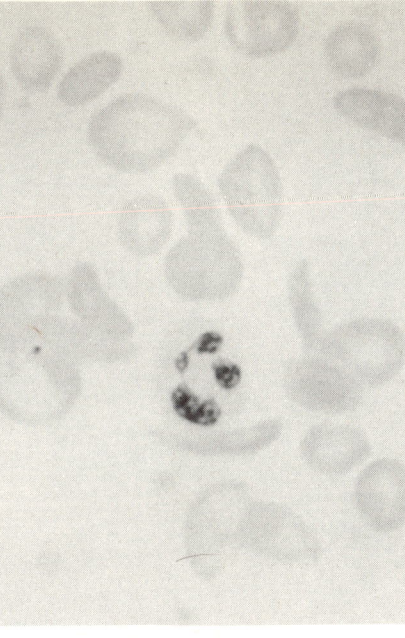 SICKLE CELL ANEMIA | 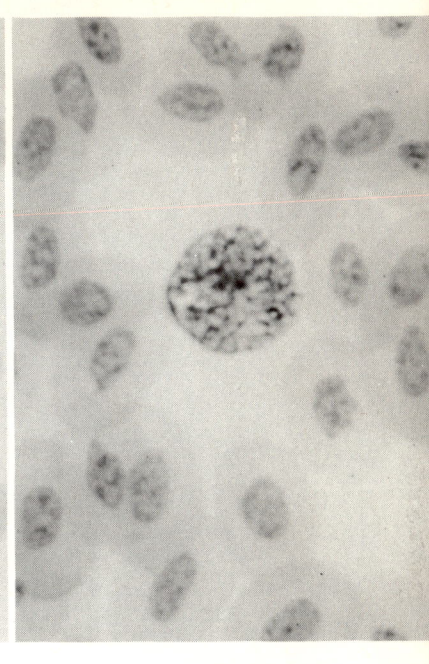 SNAKE BLOOD |

lished for hemoglobin A are abnormal and at least one is lethal. In most of them a single amino acid had been substituted. When hemoglobins from different species are compared, considerable variation appears. The significance of this variability is, of course, unknown. But the data from man suggests that each hemoglobin is precisely tailored to function in the red cells of the species in which it is found. It would probably not function in the red cells of another kind of animal.

We see, then, that the β chain from human hemoglobin, or any other polypeptide, is a most improbable molecule. Since there are twenty different kinds of amino acids to choose from, a polypeptide chain of 146 amino acids could be put together in 20^{146} ways. To simplify the figure and to allow for possible adjustments made by natural selection, let's assume that a much smaller number of possible combinations exist, perhaps 10^{146}; that is, 100,000,000,-000,000,000,000,000,000,000,000,000,-000,000,000,000,000,000,000,000,000,-000,000,000,000,000,000,000,000,000,-000,000,000,000,000,000,000,000,000,-000,000,000,000,000,000. The evidence indicates that only one, or at most a very few, of these would function properly in any given species.

Like the proteins, the nucleic acids are also long chains of smaller molecules. The units from which nucleic acid molecules are built are called nucleotides. In a nucleic acid molecule the nucleotides are strung together in the same way as are the amino acids in a polypeptide chain. There are two classes of nucleic acid. One is deoxyribonucleic acid and the other is ribonucleic acid, called DNA and RNA.

Just four different nucleotides enter into the composition of DNA—adenine, thymine, guanine, and cytosine; or A, T, G, C. For RNA the nucleotides are adenine, uracil, guanine and cytosine or A, U, G, C. In living systems DNA is for information storage and RNA for information retrieval.

Five billion nucleotide pairs of human DNA—an outstanding example of miniaturization.

In an automatic machine, information is often stored in the form of holes punched
(Please turn to page 74.)

DNA
(DEOXYRIBONUCLEIC ACID)

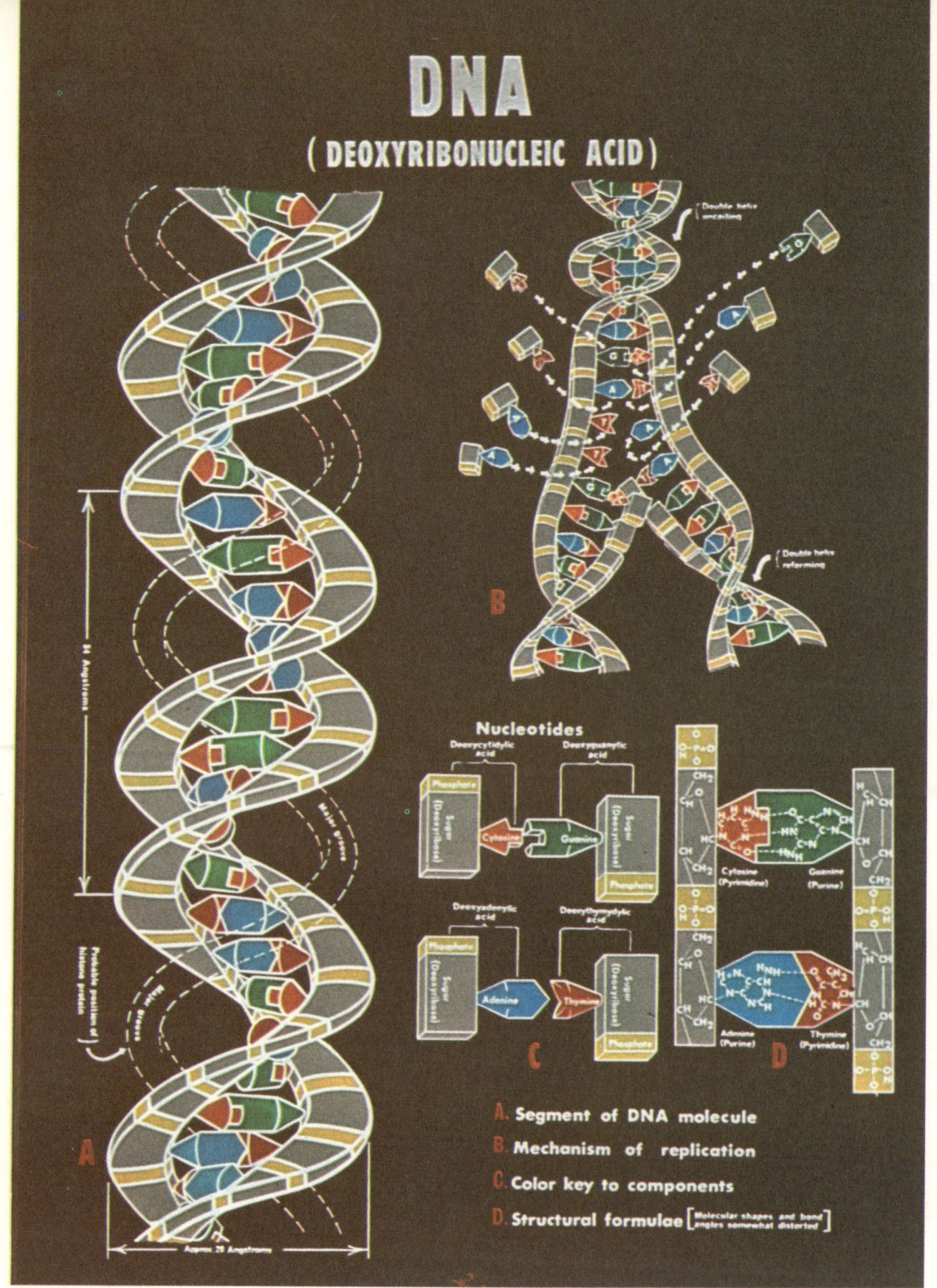

A. Segment of DNA molecule
B. Mechanism of replication
C. Color key to components
D. Structural formulae [Molecular shapes and bond angles somewhat distorted]

COURTESY CCM: GENERAL BIOLOGICAL, INC.: CHICAGO

DNA, the remarkable chemical substance that can reproduce itself, makes life on earth possible. The molecule splits, like a zipper coming undone, and nucleotides attach themselves to both halves, forming two identical molecules where there was only one. If the five billion nucleotide pairs of human DNA were strung together into a single molecule, it would be five feet long and one ten-millionth of an inch in diameter.

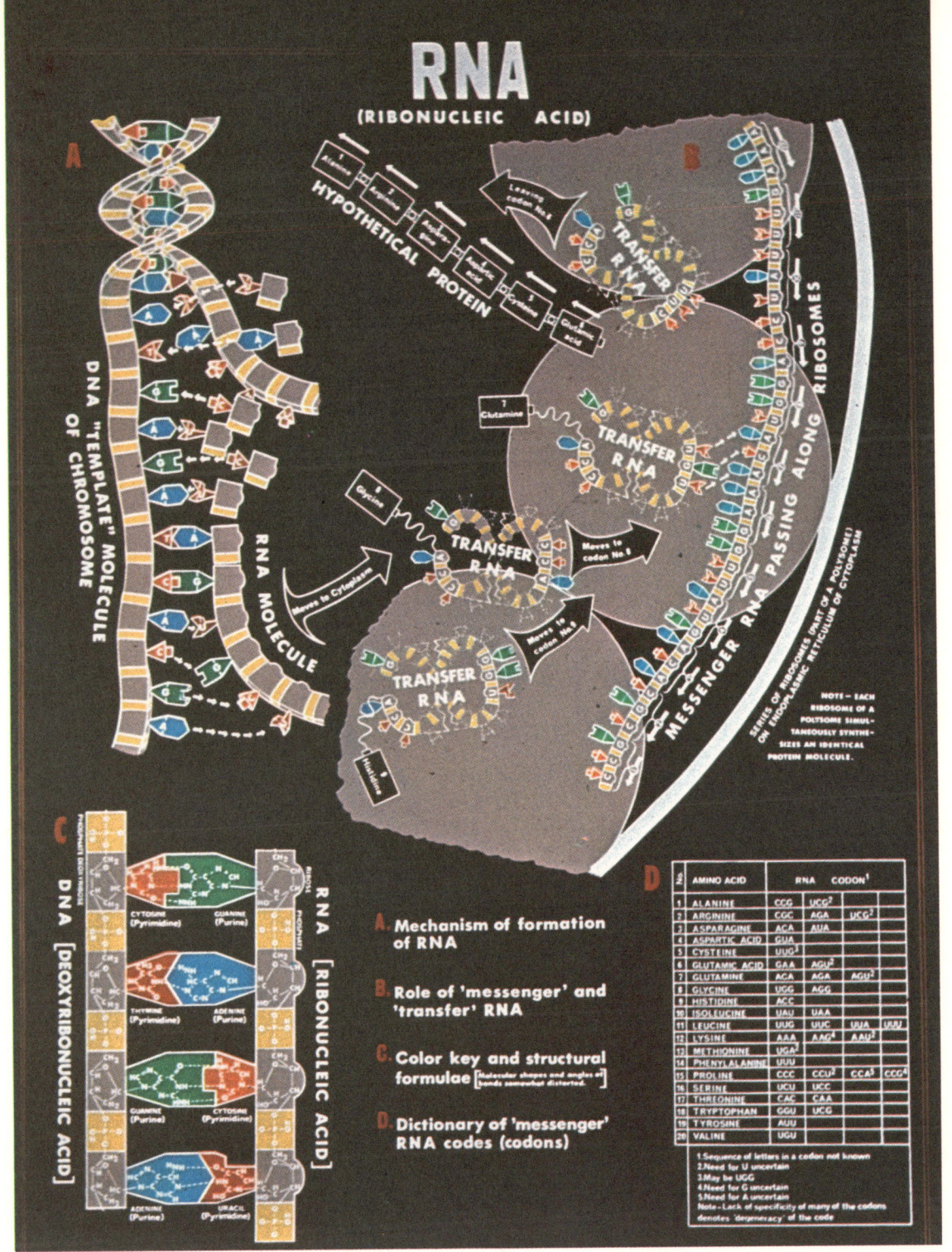

DNA also produces a substance called "messenger RNA" which carries the blueprints to make proteins; and "transfer RNA" to bring amino acids to the assembly line. For a cell to make a single protein, the following must be present: one DNA strand, twenty-two kinds of RNA, nine kinds of nucleotides, twenty kinds of amino acids, and at least twenty-four kinds of enzymes. All of this represents an inconceivably complex miniaturized computer-like operation.

in a paper tape or in a series of cards. The information is retrieved and translated into action by the intricate mechanisms of the machine. In living machines (cells), information is stored in DNA molecules by means of the sequence of the four nucleotides that make up these molecules. Actually each polypeptide constituent of all of the enzymes and other proteins of the cell is coded for by a specific section of a DNA chain which is called a gene. A sequence of *three* nucleotides on a DNA chain codes for a specific amino acid and is called a codon. Each codon codes for one of the twenty amino acids. This means that the precise sequence of amino acids in the β chain of human hemoglobin is due to a precise sequence of at least three times 146 nucleotides in the gene responsible for its synthesis. (There is more than one codon for some of the amino acids).

The amount of information coded in the DNA of an organism is amazing. The information in a single cell of human DNA is estimated as equivalent to 1,000 printed volumes, with 600 pages per volume and 500 words per page. If the estimate is correct, this is what it would take to record the complete specifications of the human body. It might be more correct, in the light of recent evidence, to compare the cell's stored information to several copies of a smaller set of books. In other words, the DNA of a human cell may contain a shorter message repeated several times. In any case the amount of information is still incredibly vast.

We hear these days about the miniaturization of electronic devices, but how about this one? If the 5,000,000,000 nucleotide pairs of human DNA were strung together into a single long molecule, it would be about five feet long and about one ten-millionth of an inch in diameter. If this molecule were folded back and forth on the head of a pin so as to make a solid film one ten-millionth of an inch thick, it would take 200 such molecules to cover the head of the pin.

To develop a new human being, gather an impressive list of raw materials and assemble a quadrillion nucleotides in sequence.

The copying process is incredibly precise. During the development of a fertilized egg into a mature human being, many cell divisions occur, and each time the "1,000 volumes" of information must be copied

The information in a single cell of DNA would fill an estimated 1,000 volumes, with 600 pages per volume and 500 words per page. Or the DNA may contain a shorter message, "a smaller set of books," repeated several times.

precisely. *This involves the assembling of an estimated 1,000,000,000,000,000 (one quadrillion) nucleotides in proper sequence.*

To make it possible for the cell to read the message on a gene and translate it into a polypeptide, an impressive amount of equipment and raw materials is necessary. In order for a cell to make a single protein the following molecules must be present: one DNA strand, twenty-two kinds of RNA, nine kinds of nucleotides, twenty kinds of amino acids, and at least twenty-four kinds of enzymes, each of which is a protein. This will result in the building of a protein *only inside* a living cell or in an experimenter's "cell-free system" which contains the cellular machinery extracted from living cells.

A maze of interrelated circuits, each part depending on others.

The amino acids and the nucleotides are put together in the cell by a step-by-step process, each step catalyzed by an enzyme. Other enzymes are necessary to build nucleotides into nucleic acids and amino acids into proteins. In other words, many proteins must be present already, before any proteins can be built. Protein synthesis, then, involves a maze of interrelated chemical circuits, and the functioning of each part depends on the proper functioning of all of the other parts.

When an archaeologist digs into the debris left by some ancient people, he has no difficulty telling an ordinary stone from an arrowhead, or a lump of clay from a pottery fragment. We can distinguish between naturally occurring objects and the works of man. To me it seems strange that scientists who can readily recognize the handiwork of strange men of ancient cultures fail to see in the marvelous complexity of living things the handiwork of the Creator.

Scientists who believe in mechanistic evolution speak of long ages of chemical evolution during which simple carbon and nitrogen compounds in the ancient lifeless seas were acted upon by heat, powerful radiations, and the like, under conditions which no longer exist. Gradually, they say, these compounds joined to form more and more complex molecules until some kind of molecular organization occurred which could reproduce itself and start life.

The probability is incredibly remote. No one has ever designed such a system in theory, let alone made it work.

It seems to me that the interdependence of DNA, three kinds of RNA, amino acids, nucleotides, and numerous enzymes in a protein-synthesizing system makes this idea preposterous. The component parts of this closed system would all have to arrive at the same point at the same time. As will be shown later, the probability of such an event is so incredibly remote as to rule it out of consideration.

Evolutionists will probably contend that a very much simpler self-duplicating system evolved during chemical evolution, and was refined during long evolution into

---

In order for a cell to make a single protein the following molecules must be present: one DNA strand, twenty-two kinds of RNA, nine kinds of nucleotides, twenty kinds of amino acids, and at least twenty-four kinds of enzymes, each of which is a protein. This will result in the building of a protein ONLY INSIDE *a living cell or in an experimenter's "cell-free system" which contains the cellular machinery extracted from living cells.*

the present system. But would the simplified system work? The facts are that no one has ever designed one in theory, let alone made it work.

Some scientists have theorized that no matter how improbable an event, given enough time it becomes inevitable. If a monkey, it is said, could be taught to punch the keys of a typewriter at random, given enough time he would produce all of the sonnets and plays of Shakespeare. A probability may be calculated for this, but it is too small to be seriously considered. Besides this, Shakespeare's works were produced by a master intelligence. Nothing in human experience justifies the conclusion that even one of his inspiring passages could be produced by chance. This example illustrates why I doubt that the "law of probability" is even applicable to the evolution of a protein-synthesizing system. Yet, to meet on their own ground those who believe in evolution, let us calculate the probability of the synthesis of one kind of polypeptide by random combinations.

The hemoglobin molecule, probability, and the number of atoms in the universe.

For this calculation we will use the β chain of the hemoglobin molecule with its 146 amino acids in sequence. If the sequence must be perfect, with no errors tolerated, the probability that any given sequence of 146 amino acids produced by random processes would be the right one is $1/20^{146}$. Let us, however, be generous and also simplify our calculations, by making the probability $1/10^{146}$. This means that a chain of 146 amino acids could be put together in 20^{146} different ways, thus producing 20^{146} kinds of polypeptide molecules. (In our simplification we are saying only 10^{146} kinds.) The number 20^{146} can also be expressed as 10^{190}, a number vastly greater than 10^{110}, the estimated number of atoms in the entire universe.

How long would it take to produce this many kinds of molecules by combinations, largely at random, of amino acids? Let us assume a vast pool of amino acids all in an activated state. Let us also assume that they are joining together at the rate of 5×10^{11} combinations per second, and that there is some mechanism present that limits the length of the chain to 146 amino acids, no more and no less. Since it requires 145 combinations to produce one molecule, this would result in about 3.4×10^9 polypeptide molecules per second.

There are about 3×10^7 (30 million) seconds per year. Let us allow 4×10^9 (four billion) years for chemical evolution. This is probably more time than anyone would claim. Our figures then are as follows:

3.4×10^9 molecules per second
3.0×10^7 seconds per year
4.0×10^9 years

Multiplying these values together we get a product of 4.0×10^{26} molecules in four billion years. Since 1×10^{146} kinds of molecules are possible, the probability that the right one would be produced in four billion years is $4 \times 10^{26} / 1 \times 10^{146}$ which equals $1/2.5 \times 10^{119}$. In other words, there is one chance in 2.5×10^{119} that the right molecule would be formed in four billion years.

Even if this unlikely event should occur, the synthesis of a single protein molecule would accomplish nothing.

In fairness it should be pointed out that 4×10^{26} molecules is a respectable sample, and it is not inconceivable that it should contain the right one. *However, the synthesis of a single protein molecule would*

Some have theorized that no matter how improbable an event, given enough time it becomes inevitable. A monkey, it is said, could in time type all the sonnets and plays of Shakespeare. But the probability for this is too small to be seriously considered. Nothing in human experience indicates that even one of Shakespeare's passages could be produced by chance.

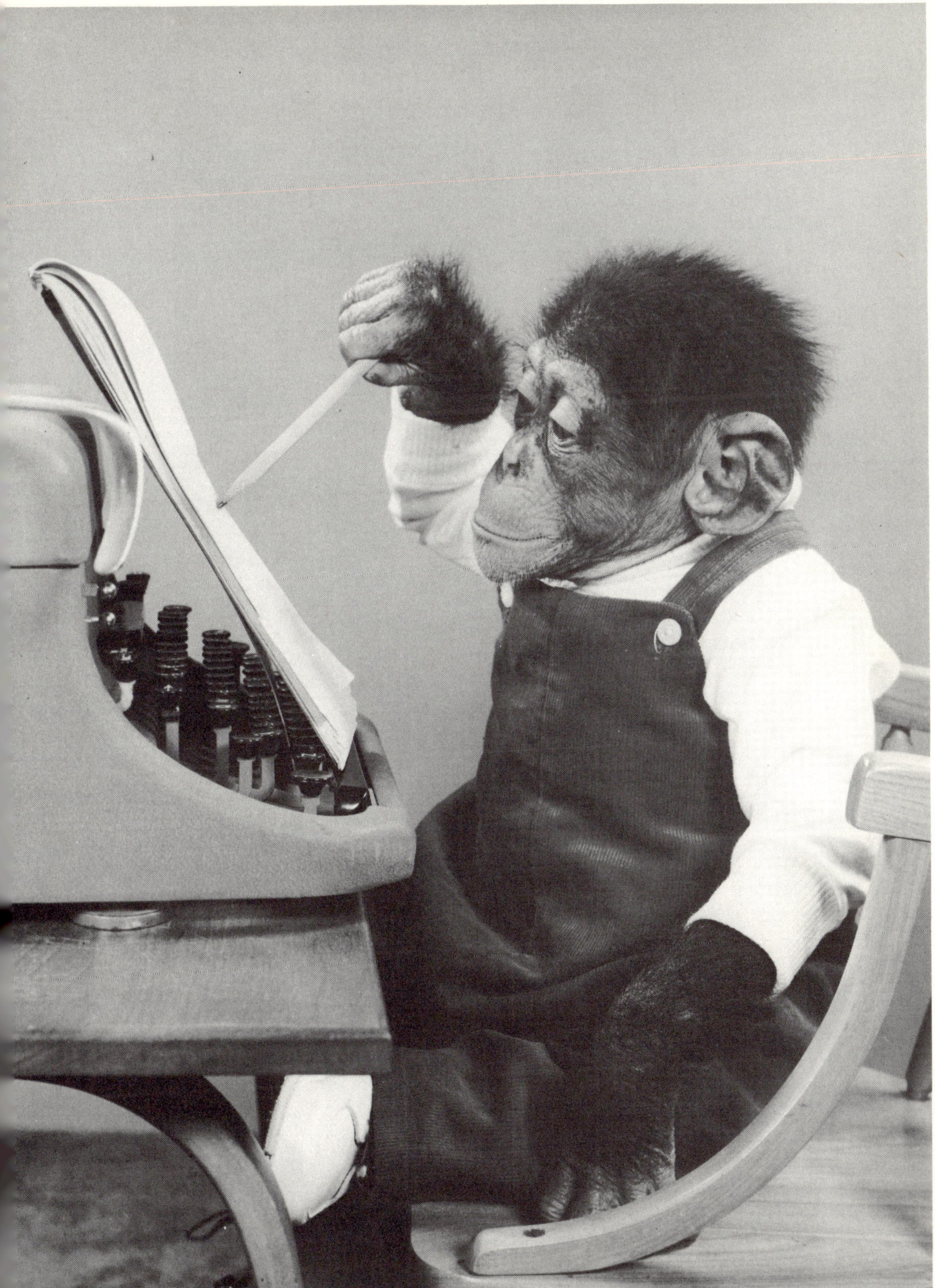

Would a RANDOM *sample of* RANDOMLY *produced molecules contain 10,000 specific biologically active enzymes?*

... It seems to me the only support for the idea of molecular evolution is to be found in the biologist's great faith in the theory of evolution.

accomplish nothing. The simplest possible protein-synthesizing system postulated by the Nobel Prize winner Lederberg requires about twenty-four different enzymes, all of which are highly specific proteins. This in addition to the DNA, the RNA's, and the various other components, all of which would have to appear at one time in one place and in the proper structural relationships.

The probability of the synthesis of one polypeptide chain by random processes is fantastically small. What shall we say then of the probability of the appearance in one place and time of the more than thirty molecules of Lederberg's "minimum chemical requirements for a hypothetical primeval organism? (See pages 36, 37.) It seems obvious that time on a geological scale is still totally inadequate to accomplish even this by random processes. And if geology does not provide us time enough for the chemical evolution of even the simplest hypothetical organism possible, where would we find the time for the development of all of the complexities of life on earth today? Remember that in the presently accepted evolutionary scheme all changes are random; all that natural selection does is to eliminate the ineffective. Natural selection would conceivably result in some economy in time, but it would not invalidate the highly conservative calculations of probability given above. It is also difficult to understand how natural selection could operate in molecular evolution.

Would a random sample of randomly produced molecules contain 10,000 specific enzymes?

Someone may object that the β polypeptide and the other highly specific proteins were not the obligatory goal of chemical evolution, but were among the ones which happened to be produced, and that from those produced over millions of years natural selection sorted out the ones which could be combined into living systems. This may look like a good argument, but consider this question: Would a *random* sample of *randomly* produced molecules contain 10,000 specific biologically active enzymes? And if it did, could they be integrated into an enzyme system capable of maintaining the life of a bacterial cell? Such a chain of circumstances seems less probable than the random synthesis of the β chain of hemoglobin.

The facts of molecular biology cry out to us that there is a God, a great Engineer, who created the natural wonders we contemplate.

It seems to me that the only support available for the idea of molecular evolution is to be found in the biologist's great faith in the theory of evolution. Personally, I find it much easier to have faith in the great Creator and in His Word. In my opinion it would be more reasonable to expect an electronic computer to develop its own programs than to assume that living cells developed theirs.

For me, at least, the above considerations effectively eliminate any mechanistic theory of evolution. Deists would probably say that matter was so created that molecular evolution was not dependent on random processes, but that the nature of matter directed the course of molecular evolution into more timesaving channels. The theistic evolutionist, on the other hand, would probably contend that God guided the course of molecular evolution. In my opinion both of these views are untenable, but since the arguments lie in the fields of theology and philosophy, they are beyond the scope of this chapter.

In conclusion, I quote Romans 1:19, 20 from the Phillips translation: "It is not that they do not know the truth about God: indeed He has made it quite plain to them. For since the beginning of the world the invisible attributes of God, for example, His eternal power and divinity, have been plainly discernible through things which He has made and which are commonly seen and known, thus leaving these men without a rag of excuse."

Surely the facts of molecular biology cry out to us that there is a God, a great Engineer who planned and executed all of the wonders which we contemplate in this scientific age.

Of necessity young animals are built along the same basic plan as their parents. Whatever the creative powers of the principle of natural selection, there are limits beyond which they cannot go.

7.

What "Natural Selection" Cannot Do

Robert E. D. Clark

In order to build up a structure by natural selection, it is essential that *each* stage in the building process must make an animal better fitted to its environment than the one before it. An eye that is half developed must be more useful to an animal than an eye that is 49 percent developed, and this, in turn, than one the development of which has proceeded to only 48 percent, and so on. The graph of usefulness against the extent of structural organization *must* show a steady upward rise—otherwise progress must inevitably stop, hindered by natural selection itself. If the graph is not a steady upward rise, but has ups and downs, then natural selection (which selects usefulness and adaptation), working from *either* direction, will force the organism to the nearest maximum.

Today, with our much greater knowledge of and familiarity with complex systems, we know that steady upward rises of the kind demanded by materialistic evolutionists are unknown to science. Isolated fundamental changes make a machine less efficient than it was before and may even make it useless, unless, indeed, numerous other adaptations are made at the same time.

The radio manufacturer cannot turn one model of set into a larger and better one by continuous stages—he cannot add a new tube, a condenser, a piece of wire, et cetera, in a series of operations, and hope each time to obtain a model that is slightly better than the one before. All the

From *The Universe: Plan or Accident?* Copyright © 1961, The Paternoster Press, Exeter, Devon, England. Used by permission.

changes must be made at once—or not at all! To add an extra tube to a radio set you must first cut through wires, disconnect the loudspeaker, et cetera, and at once the set becomes useless as a functioning whole. Only after passing through the *useless* stage can it be made more useful than before. It is the same with all arrangements of matter organized as functioning units. To ask for a gradual, uniform improvement is, it seems, to ask for the impossible.

Now, many biologists have long suspected that precisely the same principle applies to nature. If it is desired to develop one organ from another the intermediate stages will, in general, be useless and so will have no survival value. The evidence of this is even more conclusive when we consider habits rather than organs. Fabre, for instance, was convinced that many of the habits of insects could never have arisen by natural selection. And the changes which are necessary if a symbiotic union is to develop between two species which, in the process, become mutually useful to one another, are such that a change in one species which did not take place simultaneously with an appropriate change in the other would achieve no useful purpose.

This difficulty, recognized by Darwin, makes it difficult to entertain the view that an undirected evolution can progressively make simple things more complex. It was confidently hoped in the nineteenth century that further progress would throw light upon the matter. It has certainly done so—but not in the sense that the Darwinians had hoped. Today evidence is accumulating that the difficulty is universal, and it has been found to confront us even in the simplest imaginable instances where the complexities and alternative explanations that have in the past been suggested as ways of evasion do not enter the picture.

The evidence provided by modern studies in genetics is here of peculiar interest. The mold *Neurospora* (commonly used in such experiments) manufactures the amino-acid arginine, and it is known that at least seven stages are involved in the synthesis of this substance. Each of these stages is dependent upon the presence of an enzyme, and each enzyme in turn depends upon the presence of a particular gene in the hereditary substance of the mold.

Now some at least, if not all, of the intermediate stages involve the production of products, such as ornithine and citrulline, which are believed to be quite useless to the mold—they are not known to serve a useful purpose in any other living organism, and they are not essential building bricks in the manufacture of proteins.

The yucca, or Spanish bayonet, cannot pollinate itself, but must depend on the yucca moth to do this. In turn, the yucca moth depends entirely on the yucca plant for food for its larvae. (A) Yucca flower, cut open. (B) Moth with pollen ball. (C) The moth lays an egg among the ovules of the plant. (D) She then pushes the pollen ball into the tip of the pistil, thus fertilizing the plant. (E) The yucca plant. Could this phenomenon—interdependence of plant and moth—have originated by natural selection? Intermediate stages would have no survival value, and would have been useless. Darwin recognized this difficulty, but hoped further discoveries would solve the problem. However, evidence is accumulating that undirected evolution cannot progressively make simple things more complex.

These enzymes and genes cannot arise by gradual evolution, step by step. In fact, no likely mechanism for this has ever been suggested.

Thus all the details are known of a long many-staged synthesis, each step of which requires the presence of a particular elaborately organized enzyme molecule which can carry out a particular reaction.

How did all these enzymes and the genes which make them arise? They cannot arise by gradual evolution, step by step, for when once an organism develops an un-necessary product, natural selection will tend to eliminate that product. No likely mechanism has ever been suggested.

The orthodox reply to this point is that useless genes are often linked with useful ones. So a favorable mutation in one direction can carry along with it, so to speak, the unfavorable mutations of another gene which are necessary preliminaries for the emergence of something new and better.

Of course this might, and doubtless does, happen now and then by chance. But as a general explanation it carries no conviction—rather the reverse. Useless random

83

changes can take place in a multitude of directions—what is there to ensure that those will be preserved which, considered in the light of *subsequent* evolutionary history, will be seen to have been useful? Besides, it is difficult to suppose that natural selection is much of a creative power if favorable mutations are bogged down by linkage with unfavorable ones. Though many biologists pay lip service to the linkage theory, many are discreetly silent; and it is difficult to believe that any think of it as other than a somewhat desperate expedient. But there is worse to follow.

Another problem—the matter of size and weight.

A consideration of elementary scientific principles leads to yet a further difficulty. Galileo realized, centuries ago, that mechanisms must have an optimum size, and his principle still holds good and forms part of our scientific heritage. As mentioned in an earlier chapter, one cannot simply imitate a small machine on a much larger or much smaller scale. There comes a point at which basic redesign is called for—the penalty being immense inefficiency.

The reason for this is that weight, which is proportional to volume, increases as the *cube* of dimensions, but surface area increases only as the square. The force which can be generated in a muscle depends upon cross section and therefore upon area, and is otherwise limited by the ultimate chemical forces between atoms. But the work required to, say, lift a land animal, will depend upon its weight. So a fly enlarged to the size of a dog will break its legs. Surface area also determines such factors as the rate at which heat can be lost and the rate of loss or gain of carbon dioxide or oxygen through membranes. But, once more, if the structure of a small animal is repeated on a larger scale, the heat which must be lost or the gases which must diffuse, will depend upon the body weight, and this increases much faster than the surface area available. So the fly the size of a dog will be unable to respire, and,

even if it manages to do so, it will get too hot.

A radically new design will be called for. But natural selection only modifies what already exists.

So if we imagine evolution as starting with small organized structures, there must come a time when, as a result of mere size increase, small naturally selected modifications will no longer prove useful. A radically new design of the organism will be called for. But, by its very nature, natural selection cannot provide for this. It can only modify what already exists; it cannot effect radical redesign.

The point is well illustrated by comparing the young of a species with the adults. In the general case young and old are built upon the same basic plan. If natural selection could so modify the young that they would, from the start, be free living creatures, able to fend for themselves, it would doubtless have done so. But we find instead that the young must often be shielded—whether inside or outside the mother's body—because they are not viable until they have reached a certain critical size. In cases where they are left relatively unprotected the survival rate is low, and this has to be balanced by large numbers.

It seems necessary to conclude that, whatever may be the creative powers that lie dormant in the principle of natural selection, there are limits beyond which they cannot go. It is misleading and untrue, then, to argue that since Darwin's day the argument from design based upon the structure of animals has lost its force. This is certainly not the case. Indeed, the argument has been greatly strengthened as a result of our much increased knowledge concerning the intricacies and wonders of organic design.

The argument from design has been greatly strengthened.

Differentiation of species is commonly attributed to evolution. However, today, with our much greater knowledge of complex systems, we know that the steady upward rises of the kind demanded by materialistic evolutionists are unknown to science. Enzymes and genes cannot arise by gradual evolution, step by step, because once an organism develops an unnecessary product, natural selection will tend to eliminate that product. No likely mechanism has been suggested.

The rabbit that runs faster than the rest is the one most likely to escape from the lynx. The others die out, and the next generation are offspring of the "fit" survivor.

8.
Fail-safe and Foolproof

Eric A. Magnusson

Men invented the wheel and the alphabet, it is true. But when we compare man's inventiveness with nature's, the contest is uneven. Try to describe the devices nature thought of first and man "invented" later, and you will fill volumes, but nature still has plenty of inventions man has never exploited.

Automation is the key word inside plant and animal cells. Nature spares no effort to ensure that things never get out of balance or out of control. She spends her best energies to make certain that her best energies are not spent needlessly. The way this happens makes the idea of "design" and a "designer" seem inevitable; all sorts of logical barriers confront us when we try to imagine how these control systems could have been developed by gradual accumulation of changes in the chromosomes. But before we describe the control systems themselves, let us take a brief look at "natural selection," so important to current ideas of evolution.

If living conditions are harsh and only a few can survive, it is the strongest or best adapted that do it. The one rabbit in a litter that runs faster than all the rest is the one most likely to escape from the lynx. The others die out. The next generation are the offspring of the "fit" survivor, and they inherit his fitness.

For natural selection to operate, nature must have something to select. There is no way to choose the fittest if all are equally fit. But, as most people know, there is plenty of variation in nature and much opportunity

Although the gene combinations are different, none are completely new. . . . Variations in nature are variations on an already existing theme. Where did the theme come from?

for nature to exercise the power of choice between the various degrees of fitness. What is not so widely known is that there are definite limits to the variation and the kind of changes that can occur in a group of plants or animals, however accurate nature's choice or however long the selection goes on. Many different gene combinations arise in the set received by any individual because that set is "shuffled" out of the two sets of genes from the parents. But although the gene combinations are different, none are completely new. Of course, the genes may undergo slight inheritable changes—mutations—but these only modify genes already there. *Variations in nature are variations on an already existing theme. Where did the theme come from?*

Enzymes without control systems would be as useless as telephones without an exchange.

As the science of molecular biology advances, we are beginning to understand some of the really important themes. Many of them require an explanation completely different from that which natural selection can provide. It is not merely that cells are more complicated than they were once thought to be or that the cell contents are more numerous. The newer discoveries force us to describe the cell and its functions in an entirely different way. No longer can we think of the cell as a bag of enzymes plus an enzyme synthesizer to produce them when supplies run out. How many enzymes there are, what they do, and how they are made—these are vital facts to know. But other things, such as the devices that control them, are more vital still. Enzymes without control systems would be as useless to their owners as telephones without a telephone exchange.

No function can be an advantage both to have and not to have. Thus no new enzyme can evolve at the same time as its control system.

The many ingenious devices used by a cell solely to control the activities of its enzymes are evidence that a cell which is only a bag of enzymes could never survive. By no known process of natural selection can both an enzyme and its repressor develop simultaneously—one for some specific task and the other to stop it from doing that task. No function can be an advantage both to have and not to have, so it follows that no new enzyme can evolve at the same time as its control system. But neither could the two have evolved separately without one appearing before the other, and the switch could not have come first. If the enzyme appeared first, then it would be uncontrolled, a most unusual situation. Moreover, enzymes and their control systems are integrated units. Their activities are coordinated, not separated. There is no evidence that they ever have been separated or that they could have appeared independently.

One of the first control systems studied in cells is the one used by a certain microbe to regulate the use of lactose, a kind of sugar found in milk. The enzymes necessary for the breakdown of lactose are produced by the cell only when lactose is actually available. These enzymes admit lactose to the cell and then split apart the two parts of this double sugar to yield single sugars which the cell can digest. Enzymes, these remarkable substances responsible for reactions in living cells, are extremely complicated, and the drain on the resources of the cell in making them is not always to be tolerated if the enzymes are not really needed.

We still do not know exactly how the cell recognizes the presence of lactose before setting about to produce enzymes to use it. But evidently it centers around a special gene called the "regulator gene." Genes are located side by side in long chains called chromosomes, and the cell "reads" the information stored in these genes by sending the chain through a decoder located within the cell. The regulator gene is decoded in the usual way, telling the cell to produce a substance called "repressor." The repressor molecule's job is to search the chromosome ahead of the decoder until it finds a site where it makes a neat fit. In doing so, a monkey wrench is thrown into the works of the decoding mechanism, preventing the next three genes from being decoded. Their corresponding enzymes are never synthesized while "repressor" is attached to that part of the chromosome which precedes them.

These three enzymes are the very ones needed for splitting lactose. If no lactose is there, they are not needed! But if lactose really is present, then "repressor" finds lactose first and sticks to it instead of looking along the chromosome. In this way "repressor" is prevented from blocking the decoding of those genes responsible for the enzymes now that they are needed for the breakdown and utilization of the lactose which is now present! Although the molecule in question has never been isolated, the "repressor" hypothesis fits the facts so well that it must be substantially true. At least, so thought a recent Nobel Prize Committee in honoring French scientists Monod and Jacob for its discovery.

An automobile needs both motor and brakes, but such a mechanism comes only from intelligent design.

One would hardly waste money on a new automobile that had no motor; but neither would one want a car, however fine, that had no brakes. Five minutes in city traffic would reduce it to twisted metal and shattered glass. Both the motor (enzyme) and the brakes (repressor) are vital. But mechanisms like this could never result from natural selection; intelligent design seems to be the only answer.

Of course, someone can always say that the genes for the utilization of lactose evolved first, and that regulation of their synthesis was a later adaptation occurring when lactose did disappear for a time long enough to permit the development of the "switch." But this would be equally unsatisfactory. The three enzymes required for utilization of lactose are clustered adjacent to one another on the chromosome. This is necessary for the operation of the switch, which works by jamming the normal decoding mechanism for that section of the chromosome immediately following the point of attachment of "repressor." If these genes happened to evolve independently of the control system, then it is inconceivable that each should have appeared in exactly the same segment of the chromosome in such a way that subsequent random changes in the section immediately preceding them should produce a "switch" affecting those three but no others. It would be even more remarkable if, during the long time that lactose was absent (a condition necessary for the development of the control system with its operator and regulator genes) no mutation or deletion or any other change affected the "lactose genes." Deletion or loss of genes or parts of them is a common enough event; surely the complete removal of the "lactose genes" would be the first thing to happen to a cell deprived of lactose; not development of a highly complicated switch.

How did the enzyme survive eons of random mutations and chromosome deletions without affecting its lactose splitting ability?

Not all control systems are like the one just described, nor is it the only one affecting lactose in the bacterial cell. The enzymes are not even synthesized unless lactose is present, but this does not ensure that they will be used even if they are synthesized. One of the components of the complex sugar lactose is the simple sugar glucose, supplies of which are often plentiful whether lactose is present or not. When glucose is already present, overproduction is avoided by another device which causes the lactose-splitting enzyme β-galactosidase to lose its activity. The device seems to

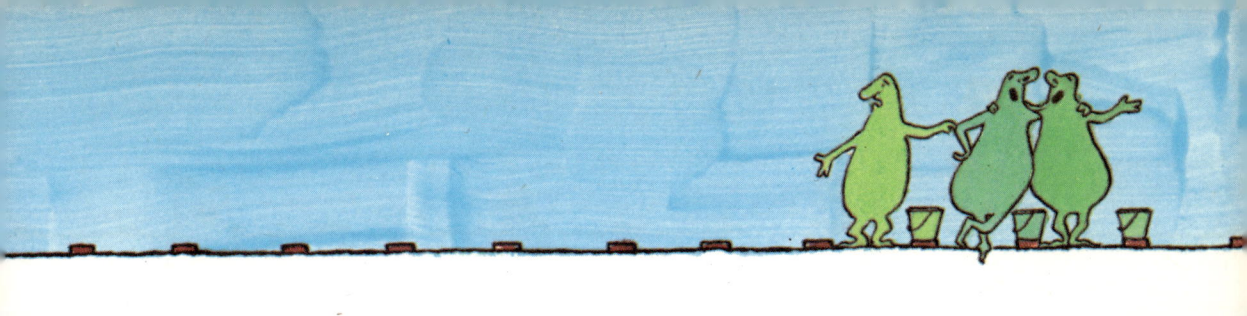

Above: Reader (red) starts along chromosome. He releases Repressor (orange), who rushes ahead and locates Lactose (yellow). Repressor joins up with Lactose.

Reader continues along chromosome until he comes to Genes. Meanwhile Repressor and Lactose walk together.

Reader, arriving where Genes are, puts them to work secreting enzymes which split Lactose into two parts, making it useful to the cell.

If Repressor finds no Lactose to join up with, he goes to the Chromosome and stops Reader from putting Genes to work.

Not only the presence of amino acids is necessary, but also close control of their concentrations. This is to ensure that functions do not become "tangled up" by overproduction or underproduction. Asking the question "Which came first?" seems only to invite the answer, "Neither!"

work like this: Glucose, when present, sticks to the lactose-splitting enzyme at a site on its surface into which it fits hand in glove. Once it is stuck there, it changes the shape of the enzyme enough to prevent its attaching itself to lactose in the normal way, and lactose is left unsplit.

Here is the dilemma again. Glucose can hardly have been absent while the enzyme developed the ability to "bind-glucose-and-be-inactivated." But if it were present, the enzyme itself would be no advantage for a cell already rich with glucose, since the end result of the enzyme's action is the production of more glucose. If the glucose-operated switch, preventing the production of more glucose in the cell, came after the development of the lactose-splitting facility of the enzyme which separates the glucose from the lactose portion, then how did the enzyme survive long eons of random mutations, chromosome deletions, and the like, without affecting its lactose-splitting ability? Surely a single mutation affecting the lactose-splitting ability would provide instantaneously a much simpler way to prevent the production of glucose than the development of a complicated system that would take millions of generations to evolve.

When you design a cell, the biggest thing is not which enzymes, but how to control them.

Biochemists can now display long lists of gene clusters automatically controlled by devices like those involved with the lactose enzymes in bacterial cells. When you are designing a cell, the biggest thing to decide is not which enzymes, but how to control them. Such decisions may be no problem to someone in a position to design cells and make prior decisions about their contents, but natural selection seems excluded as the explanation for the ones already here. It is very hard to eliminate *design*.

In one organism the genes for the set of ten enzymes needed for synthesizing the amino acid histidine (an important building block needed for making enzymes) are also arranged in a line along the chromosome and all are switched off when this building block is already present in the cell. It is only when the building block is unavailable in the food supply that the enzymes need to be synthesized so that the cell's need of histidine can be supplied by the cell itself.

What of the original improvement by which the crucial function first came about?

Histidine is just one of twenty amino acids which cells require for the construction of enzymes and other proteins. Some organisms can synthesize all of them, but many need to obtain at least some of them from the food supply. If functioning cells already possess an enzyme system for producing amino acids, it is easy to talk about the modifications and possible improvements by random mutations and other changes in the genes. But what of the original improvement by which the crucial function first came about?

Take the enzymes that synthesize the amino acid leucine. Without leucine they could not exist. It is an essential component of all of them. But if it is present, what is

92

the value of a set of enzymes to produce more of what is already in constant and adequate supply?

The control systems actually in operation display remarkable economy as well as precision.

The problem is not solved by proposing that primitive cells developed in an environment rich in all the various necessary building blocks—amino acids. This only postpones the problem. In addition, quite apart from the almost impossible demands this places on the types of compounds available in the imagined primeval environment, there is the complication that not only the presence of amino acids is necessary, but also close control of their concentrations. In nature at present, this is achieved by many finely developed control systems ensuring that the many hundreds of different functions simultaneously performed by the cell do not become "tangled up" by overproduction or underproduction of any one substance. Asking the question, "Which came first?" seems only to invite the answer, "Neither!"

The control systems actually in operation display remarkable economy as well as precision. In the mold *Neurospora crassa* the amino acids valine and isoleucine are made by the action of the same set of four enzymes acting on different raw materials. An additional set of four enzymes acts on one of the intermediates of one of the production lines to produce a third amino acid, leucine. A very carefully designed control system operates here. If isoleucine is present in the cell in adequate amounts, then enzyme No. 1 is still produced, but its function is inhibited in some way. It is suggested that a molecule of isoleucine snaps onto each enzyme molecule, thus distorting the enzyme so that its usual function is no longer performed. The other production lines are affected in the same way if their end products are already available. Only the first enzyme in a production line is affected—this is all that is necessary. However, when all three amino acids are available, the cell stops manufacturing the nine enzymes altogether. If leucine alone is present, enzymes 6, 7, 8, and 9 alone are repressed, and production of the other two amino acids continues.

One final example: Glutamine is a substance used in a wide variety of organisms as raw material for the manufacture of other more complicated substances. Often eight of these other products are dependent on the glutamine supply. It is obviously necessary to obtain adequate supplies of such a vital substance, but it is also important to prevent its overproduction. If any of the eight substances are present already, the production of glutamine is slightly repressed; if two are abundant, it is further repressed, and so on. If all eight are abundant, the production line is shut down completely!

Could the complex series of checks and balances have arisen by gradual accumulation of changes in the chromosomes?

The collections of enzymes found in cells today are necessary for their very existence, but only because they are controlled. Is it conceivable that there once was a cell in which the control systems were absent? Even granting that there could have been, is it possible that the complex series of checks and balances that now exists could have arisen by gradual accumulation of changes in the chromosomes? If so, how could the requirements of the natural selection theory, that each change be beneficial, be met? How could the conditions necessary for developing the "switched-on" enzyme avoid conflict with those for developing the device that switches it off? Lactose cannot be both present and absent.

Why multiply hypotheses? It is wise to consider the alternative—a Designer.

When we come to such an impasse, it is wise to consider the alternative—that of a Designer. Why multiply hypotheses about which came first, the enzyme or the on-off switch? It is not a necessary principle of scientific inquiry, but merely a habit of thought, to insist that the complex must always be derived from the simple.

What happened to automobiles may well have happened to cells. Today's limousine survives the competition of its rivals by inheriting the features that made its predecessor survive and then adding its own innovations. But the first automobile was not produced like that. It was invented, not derived; it was the product of a mind.

And if this be true of cells, it is worth pointing out that the mind that designed them will be at least as different from the minds that design horseless carriages as are the products of their design. One attracts interest, perhaps even adulation, but the other is awe-inspiring.

Natural selection favors the fittest creatures, and the next generation inherits the slight changes.

Upper left: Thanks to protective coloration, this phasmid lived in the same tree with a hungry shrike family, escaping detection.

Upper right: Red underwing moth on lichen-covered bark.

Lower left: Camouflage helps horned lizard survive. Lower right: Katydid on spice bush leaf, both with dicot venation. Variations in nature are abundant; she has many opportunities to exercise the power of choice. But there are definite limits to the kinds of changes that can occur. Variations in nature are variations on an already existing theme. Where did the theme come from?

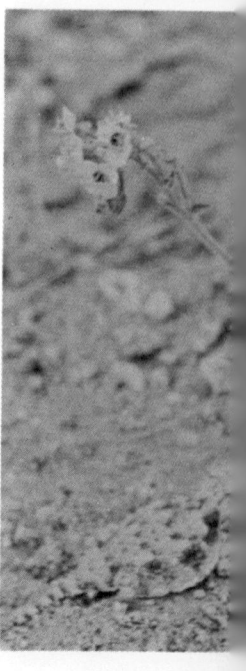

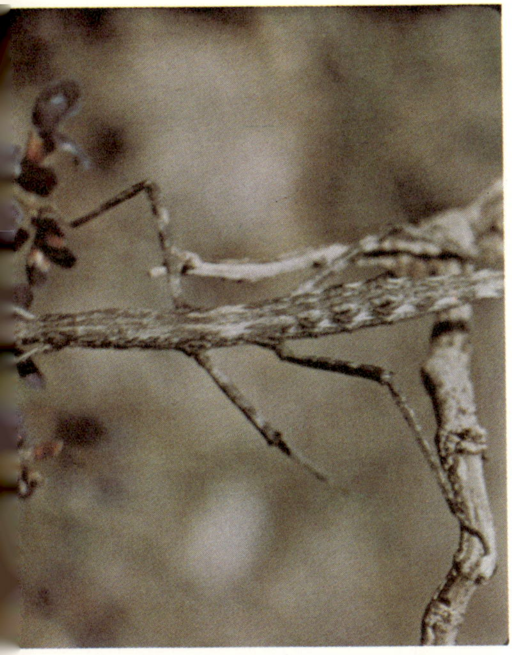

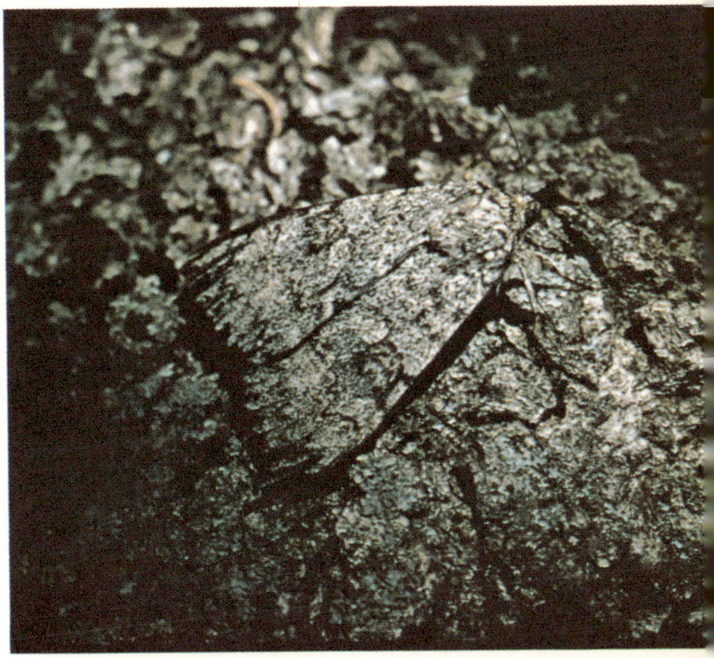

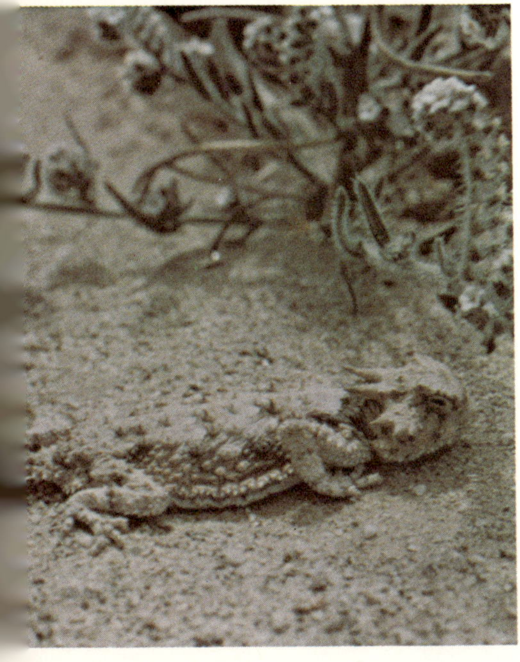

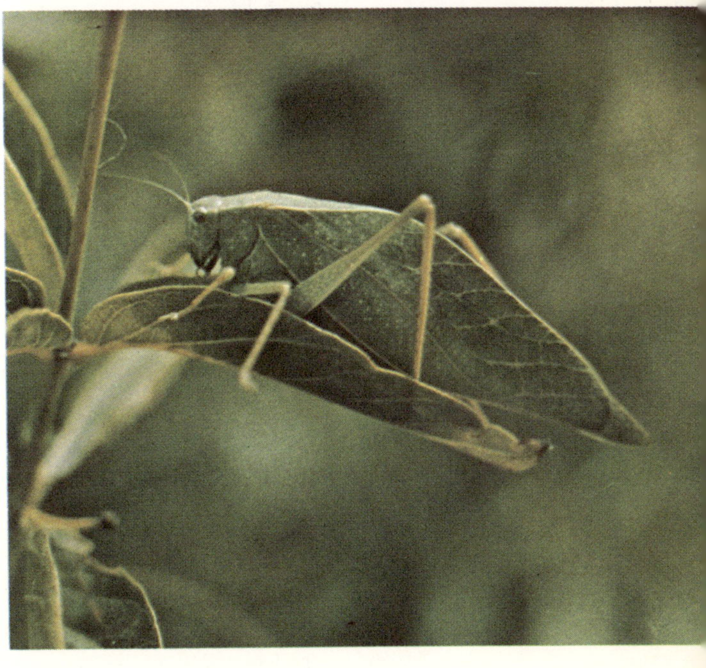

To "Consider the lilies of
the field, how they grow," we now
add, Consider the stars and
how they are transformed

9.
Modern Science: An Enlarging Vista

James R. Van Hise

In the past men caught glimpses of God's ways from the green fields, the lofty trees, the colorful flowers, the balancing of the clouds, the beating of ocean waves on the coast. Christ Himself spoke in parables of trees, birds, flowers, and hills. Indeed, these must be some of the best means by which we learn of God's will and ways.

If these readily apparent aspects of nature lead us to truths concerning God, may not other aspects of nature, not as apparent, do so as well?

A man who is both deaf and blind must depend on the senses of smell, taste, and touch for all he knows of the world around him. But if this man should be given the use of his ears, the realm of sound opens around him. He is able to understand his environment more completely. Should this man be given the use of his eyes also, the realm of light and color opens to him. He is then able to formulate even more complete ideas of his surroundings. He now has the capability to investigate aspects of reality previously denied him.

In a similar way scientific equipment and methods broaden our concept of our total environment. Magnification extends our perception of objects. Magnifying lenses date back to the Assyrians living before the time of Christ. In various stages the microscope was developed as a tool enabling the biologist to place lower and lower limits on the size of known living things. With the field ion microscope physicists have been able to see such small things as individual atoms.

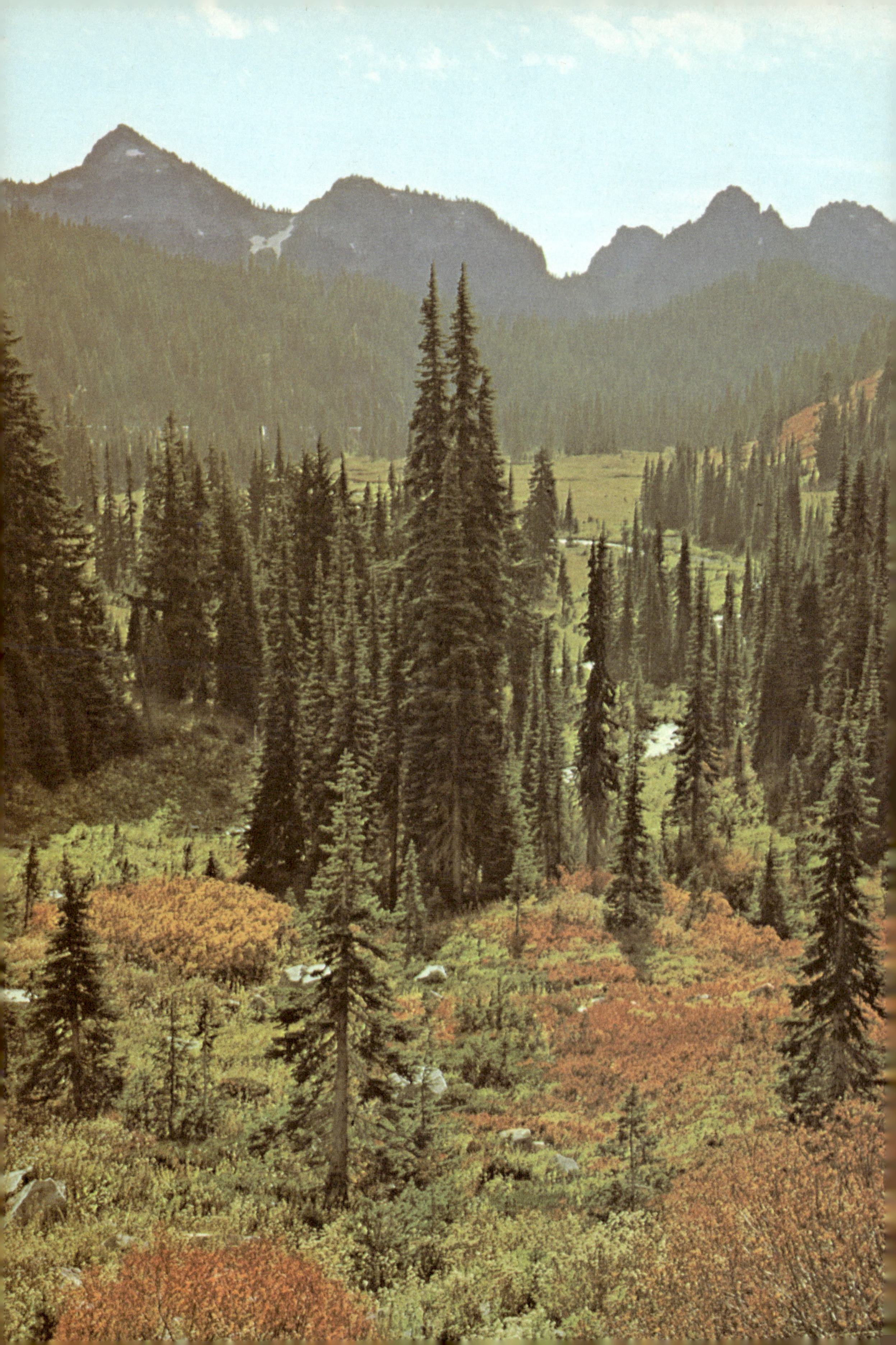

The development of the telescope began with Galileo Galilei. Using modern telescopes astronomers have been able to chart the orbits of planets and view distant stars and galaxies. At the same time, larger and larger limits have been placed on the known size of the universe we live in. With the development of more sensitive photographic emulsions it became possible to gain not only information of motion and size, but detailed information on the composition of space and the bodies of the universe. Recent sophisticated electronic methods now obtain information on composition of heavenly bodies which was not possible even by use of photographic emulsion.

These new insights speak at least as strongly of a Designer as the obvious sight of flowers, trees, and clouds.

These and hundreds of other recent developments have gradually allowed man to probe secrets of nature not previously known. Most of what we know about the detailed ways of nature has come within

All living plants depend on the infinitesimal chlorophyll molecule and the carbon atom with its unique properties. And life depends no less on the huge sun, 93 million miles away, with its many wavelengths of radiant energy.

this century. The rapid advancement of such tools has not been very different from the parable of the deaf and blind man who gradually gained hearing and sight. In this century scientists have entered a domain previously closed. These new insights speak at least as strongly of a Designer as the obvious sight of flowers, trees, and clouds. As new tools and techniques arise in science, we may appreciate God on the basis of more sophisticated evidence than ever before. It may be argued that physics and chemistry, the sciences lying closer to the fundamental basis of all matter, have been affected by evil to a smaller degree than the sciences which deal with life processes. Thus it is conceivable that, at the present, the inanimate aspects of nature may reveal a more accurate picture of certain qualities of the Designer than the animate.

I do not imply that the existence of God can be proved. God cannot be put into a test tube. It is not possible adequately to describe that which exists beyond the necessity of matter and dimension. As LeComte du Nouy puts it in *Human Destiny*: "If we could really conceive God, we could no longer believe in Him because our representation being human, would inspire us with doubts." He further points out that "it is not the image we create of God which proves God. It is the effort we make to create this image." From the facts at our disposal we can only derive a rational basis for faith, but that in itself is an enterprise worthy of our best energies.

To get at some of the really deep secrets of nature, consider the basic building blocks, the atoms. Carbon, atom number six in the periodic table, is the "backbone" of all plants and animals. It is the principal element making up the structural material in plants. It has the ability to form bonds to other carbon atoms. Thousands of these atoms may be linked to each other to form long chains.

The chlorophyll molecule, capturing the sun's radiant energy, uses it to make other useful organic molecules.

One molecule, the chlorophyll molecule, which contains many carbon atoms, is mostly responsible for capturing the radiant energy of the sun and for using it to make other useful organic molecules. If it were not for the sun's radiant energy bathing the earth, life could not exist. Light from the sun is a form of energy. Living things use this energy to manufacture organic molecules of which all living things are made.

The range of the radiant energy pervading the universe is tremendous, measuring from 0.001 angstrom to 10^{13} (or 10,000,000,000,000) angstroms.[1] The upper range of wavelength shown is 10^{16} (or 10,000,000,000,000,000) times larger than the lower range. The range of wavelengths is divided into parts labeled from gamma rays (short wavelengths and high energy) to radio waves (long wavelengths and low energy).

Light comprises the wavelengths designated by the visible range. That is, the range of wavelengths of electromagnetic radiation which we can detect ("see") with our eyes we call "light." If we should represent the entire range of electromagnetic radiation on a proportional scale short enough to be comprehensible, the range of visible wavelengths (light) would be so narrow that unless expanded many times the "visible" range could not even be seen.

Animals, people, and, remarkably, plants can "see" in this small portion of the total range of energy.

This small portion of the total range of energy extends from approximately 3,800 to 7,600 angstroms. This is the region in which animals as well as humans can see. Remarkably enough, it is also the region in which plants can "see"; that is, it marks the range of wavelengths which can be used by plants to manufacture food for life. Actually, the range of wavelengths which plants can use, from 3,000 to 7,100 angstroms, is slightly wider than the visible range. Waves outside of this range no eye can see, no plant can use. Yet it is just within this range that our sun gives 75 percent of its radiation energy.

The element carbon is the "backbone" of all living things, plant and animal. Simple organic molecules (opposite) show how carbon atoms join together to make organic chemicals. Top to bottom: acetic acid (vinegar); ethyl alcohol; butyl mercaptan (skunk essence); glucose (simple sugar); and vitamin C. Black represents a carbon atom; green, oxygen; light gray, hydrogen; dull green, sulphur.

1. An angstrom is both a measure of energy and a unit of length. Equal to one two hundred fifty-four millionths (1/254,000,000) of an inch, it is used to indicate light-wave lengths and atomic dimensions.

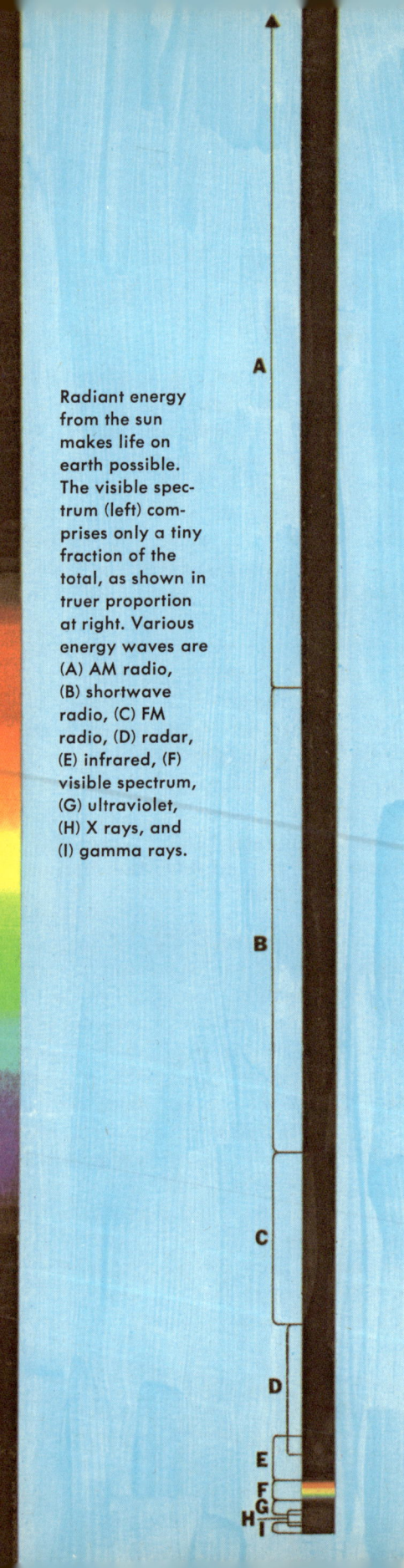

Radiant energy from the sun makes life on earth possible. The visible spectrum (left) comprises only a tiny fraction of the total, as shown in truer proportion at right. Various energy waves are (A) AM radio, (B) shortwave radio, (C) FM radio, (D) radar, (E) infrared, (F) visible spectrum, (G) ultraviolet, (H) X rays, and (I) gamma rays.

Chlorophyll absorbs blue and red light, leaving green as the light that meets our eyes.

The molecule most responsible for capturing and converting the radiant energy of the sun, the chlorophyll molecule, absorbs wavelengths best at 4,300 and 6,500 angstroms. The maximum absorption peaks are near blue at the short wavelengths and red at the long wavelengths. The light reflected from leaves of plants, therefore, lacks red and blue, leaving green as the light which meets our eyes.

The structure of chlorophyll provides us with an insight into this remarkable molecule. The part of the molecule responsible for absorbing light is called the porphyrin ring. The outside of this molecular ring is composed mainly of carbon atoms. Only the unique properties of the carbon atom allow this ring to exist and be stable. In fact, the same atomic bonds that give such great stability to the chlorophyll molecule also allow for the absorption of light.

We begin to appreciate how narrow are the margins that allow for the existence of life.

The sunlight spectrum is exceptionally well suited to sustaining life. If, relative to the entire electromagnetic spectrum, it should shift by only an infinitesimal amount, life as we know it could not exist.[2] We now begin to appreciate how very precise are the many parameters which allow for the existence of life, how narrow the margins. Very small changes in any one of them could extinguish life on earth. The apparent improbability that circumstances favorable to life could happen by chance is staggering. We are impressed that

---

2. It has been argued that the chlorophyll molecule evolved into its present structure after all other trial structures failed (their absorption spectra not being coincident with the sunlight and therefore leaving them without survival value). However, given the present forces in the atoms, no molecule which is both stable and capable of carrying out the kinds of functions necessary for a complex living organism, could absorb effectively very far in the spectra from where the chlorophyll molecule does.

This solar-energy-powered factory illustrates what a leaf—any leaf—accomplishes with the aid of chlorophyll. (1) The radiant energy absorber transforms sunlight into a form of energy which splits water (2) into hydrogen (3) and oxygen (4). Carbon dioxide (5) joins hydrogen in chemical synthesis chamber (6) which leads to the formation of carbohydrates such as sugar (7). Excess water is eliminated (8) but through nature's water cycle eventually returns (2) to enter into plant life again, repeating the process.

surely a cosmic Architect was at work to design and is at work to sustain. We are led to agree with Job: "Lo, these are parts of His ways."

But we only begin to appreciate the wonder of our environment if we confine our attention to the planet. Our sun, for example, is only one of about 30,000 to 100,000 million[3] stars in our galaxy called the Milky Way. And there are millions of galaxies separated from each other by millions of light years. Our galaxy is some 100,000 light years or 600,000,000,000,-000,000 miles in diameter. This span is so large we cannot conceive of it. Yet astronomers have been able to observe celestial bodies millions of light years away, far beyond our own galaxy.

Astronomers learn about the composition of stars by analyzing their emitted light. Since, as previously noted, the radiation from the sun and all stars is composed of many different wavelengths, astronomers, using a spectroscope, are able to separate the radiation into its various wavelengths. The principle of the spectroscope is illustrated with a prism. Light entering a prism separates, violet corresponding to the shortest wavelengths and red corresponding to the longest.

Since each element has its own unique set of wavelengths in which it absorbs radiation, a typical star spectrum, showing all the spectral lines from the elements which make it up, is quite complex. The sun shows such a spectrum.

By accurately measuring the wavelengths of the spectral lines emitted, it is possible to learn what elements make up a star. Significantly, astronomy has discovered that the stars, as far as can be determined by the spectrograph, are made of the same elements found on earth.

Interestingly enough, helium was discovered in the spectrum of the sun by the British astronomer Norman Lockyer before it was detected on the earth.

---

3. There are portions of our galaxy we cannot see well.

The universe is made of the same atoms as the earth, as we might expect.

The apparently insignificant fact that all we see in the universe is made of the same atoms as are found on the earth tells us that the laws we find in force here on earth are the same as far as we can see. Such a general applicability of the laws of nature is what we might expect in a universe run by a universal Designer.

The Crab nebula exhibits another example of the universality of the laws of nature. In A.D. 1054 the Chinese and Japanese recorded an exploding bright star (supernova) which could be seen by the naked eye for some time after it was first seen and was so bright that it was visible in the daytime for several months. Eventually its intensity decreased so that today it can be seen only with the largest telescopes. What is left is called the Crab nebula. A good share of the light from the Crab is what we call synchrotron radiation. This type of radiation was discovered here in *earthbound* laboratories, using machines called synchrotrons.

Essentially, the sun is a stupendous hydrogen bomb.

Stars are enormously hot and emit tremendous amounts of energy. Astronomers soon understood that our sun's fiery display, as well as that of other stars, could not result from ordinary chemical burning, such as of coal or oil, since they would have burned out long ago. We now understand that the sun's energy results from *nuclear* burning. Made primarily of hydrogen, the simplest element, the sun contains smaller quantities of the heavier elements. In its interior nuclear reactions continuously transform hydrogen into the heavy elements. In this nuclear transformation process, enormous amounts of energy are given off. Essentially, the sun is a stupendous hydrogen bomb. Yet most of this energy is given off in the form of radiation in the range of the spectrum useful to plants and animals.

Hence, we conclude that the sun and other stars are the generating sources for elements in the universe. But at the same time they produce light of just the right wavelengths necessary for life to exist. To me it is truly remarkable that the same complex processes which produce the most basic building blocks in the universe, the atoms, also sustain the most complex processes in the universe, life itself!

In the physical universe diverse and apparently unrelated processes work together for the good, indeed, for the very existence, of each other. At the same time these processes depend so delicately on so many variables that we exclaim: "The heavens declare the glory of God; and the firmament showeth His handiwork."

The more we learn, the more we see of the intricacy and beauty of nature, and the more we see of the wisdom of the Creator.

Our learning something about God's creation does not in any way decrease our concept of God's power or glory. To know a little about the mystery of creation does no harm to it. Nor does a little knowledge about creation make unnecessary the Creator. On the contrary, it tells us more of the power and glory of the Designer. The more we learn, the more we see of the intricacy and beauty of nature—and the more we see of the power and wisdom of the Creator, who exercises continuous and instantaneous control over the forces in nature. God is the One who binds "the sweet influences of Pleiades" and guides "Arcturus with his sons," and knows "the ordinances of heaven."

To "Consider the lilies of the field, how they grow," we now add, Consider the stars and how they are transformed.

To me it is truly remarkable that the same complex processes which produce the most basic building blocks in the universe, the atoms, also sustain the most complex processes in the universe, life itself!

To know a little about the mystery of creation does no harm to it. Nor does a little knowledge about creation make unnecessary the Creator.

Three distinct sea creatures, a sea anemone, a coral, and a starfish, share an ocean-floor habitat. Early followers of Darwin expected that gaps between such diverse kinds of living creatures would soon be filled, but it has long been apparent that such links are conspicuously absent.

10.
Those Missing Links

Richard M. Ritland

"If evolution is true, fossil history will reveal a branching plan for the advance of life, with each branch showing gradual improvement for its particular mode of existence." So says Julian Huxley in *The Wonderful World of Life,* a superbly illustrated book for children. At the top of the page is a diagram showing various kinds of animals springing from the same ancestor. Each branch in the picture has broad connections with the trunk.

Are there branches like this in the fossil record? Do they really connect? Or are there major gaps—missing links—between the main branches of life?

To understand what is meant by the "tree of life" or "missing links," we need to see how plants and animals are classified. A little over two centuries ago naturalists began trying to arrange the countless kinds of plants and animals in some kind of order. They finally adopted a system which owes most to the efforts of Linnaeus, a great Swedish naturalist.

This is how it works. First we have species of living things, like the apple tree, the sugar pine, the African elephant, the snow leopard, the bald eagle, and the human being. There are more than a million different species. Members of a species share characteristics that make them different from other groups, and they can interbreed to produce offspring. Species usually remain distinct from one another in nature. Several varieties, or races, may occur within a species. Different kinds of dogs, of horses, and of men are examples of this.

Cat species like the African lion, mountain lion, Bengal tiger, and jaguar all belong to the genus called *Felis*. Trees such as the sugar pine, yellow pine, lodgepole pine belong to the genus *Pinus*. Different genera (plural of genus) which resemble each other are grouped together in families. The pine tree genus with over 120 species, the fir tree genus with many species, the cedar of Lebanon genus with three species, and some others, are all placed in the pine family, *Pinaceae*. Families are brought together in orders, orders in classes, classes in phyla or divisions. Finally, there is the *animal kingdom* and the *plant kingdom*.

The trunk of the "tree of life" would be the kingdom; the major branches, phyla; and smaller branches, classes, orders, families, and genera; the smallest branches would be the species. According to the theory of evolution, each species would develop from evolutionary ancestors or parent species.

If we could gather in one place all of the animals and plants that ever lived, we should have, according to the theory of evolution, one continuous array of living forms. From the simple ancestors there should be intergradations to all the present-day types, because evolution is said to progress from one type to another by many small changes. The genus, family, order, and class would be arbitrary, since all groups would merge as they went back in time. Life would form a continuously varying mosaic without missing links or gaps.

Early followers of Darwin optimistically forecast that the gaps would soon be filled in. They expected that the study of deep-

In all of nature the kinds of living things are distinct one from the other. There is no known continuous sequence from one order to another.

Perhaps the most natural explanation is that the missing links between major groups never existed.

sea life, then almost unknown, would provide many of the still-living links; and the fossil record should supply more missing links.

Has their expectation been rewarded? No. Unfortunately for Darwin's theory, the results on both counts have proved bitterly disappointing. "It has now long been apparent that such links are, in fact, conspicuous by their absence," says the historian Charles Singer.

Take, for example, the phylum which includes sea lilies, starfish, sea urchins, and other sea creatures. Ancient members of this phylum are commonly believed to be the evolutionary parents of backboned animals—fish, reptiles, birds, and mammals. But the difference between the two groups is striking. The gap is so large that scientists disagree as to whether this phylum or some other, such as the segmented worms, were the ancestors.

Hereditary changes (mutations) ordinarily make small, sometimes almost imperceptible, differences. If one creature evolved from the other, there should be not one, but hundreds or thousands of intermediate steps. There should be, not a single link, but a series of links or steps. Those halfway between, or one-fourth or three-fourths of the way along the road, should not fit into either phylum. Even if the intermediates are extinct, we might expect a few of the connecting links to be preserved as fossils.

But this is not what the fossil record shows, either in the starfish or other kinds of animals or plants. Says A. H. Clark, authority on marine fossils: "One of the most striking and important facts which have been established through a study of the fossil animals is that from the very earliest times, from the very first beginnings of the fossil record, the broader aspects of the animal life upon the earth have remained unchanged.

Fossils are quickly recognized as members of a group.

"When we examine a series of fossils of any age, we may pick out one and say with confidence, 'This is a crustacean,' or a starfish, or a brachiopod, or an annelid, or any other type of creature as the case may be.

"How do we recognize these fossils as members of the various groups? We are able to recognize them because they fall within the definition of a particular group. But the definitions of the phyla or major groups of animals are all drawn up on the basis of a study of the living representatives alone.

Throughout the fossil record the major groups have remained essentially unchanged.

"Since all the fossils are determinable as members of their respective groups by the application of definitions of those groups drawn up from and based entirely on living types, and since none of these definitions of the phyla or major groups of animals need be in any way altered or expanded to include the fossils, it naturally follows that throughout the fossil record these major groups have remained essentially unchanged. This means that the interrelationships between them likewise have remained unchanged."[1]

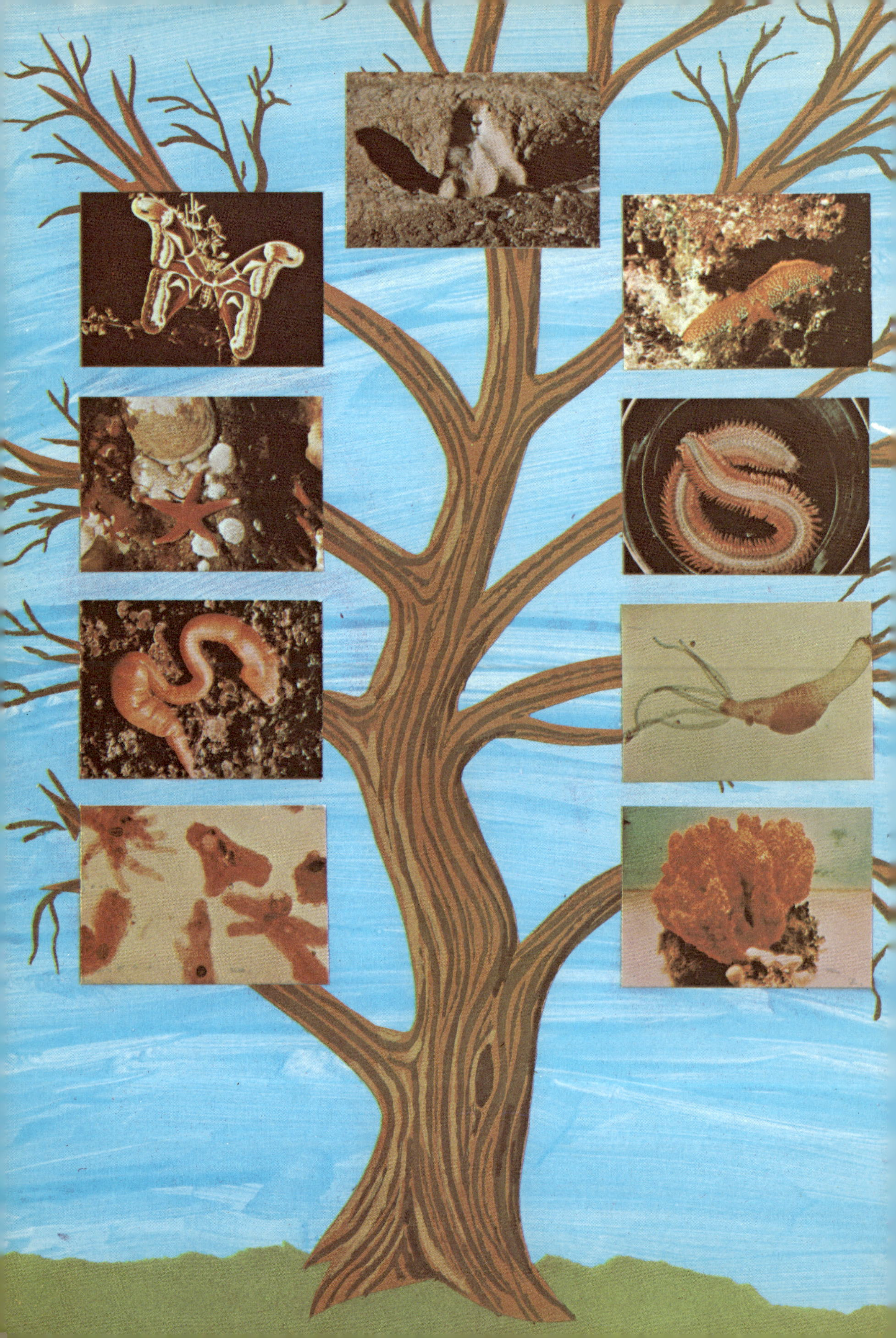

Typical charts in children's science books show broad connections in the "evolutionary tree." But more accurate textbooks usually show these connections as dotted lines. The evolutionary connections are speculative only, and not supported by fossils. The large branches in evolutionary "trees" are held together only by theory. To some thoughtful students, these problems make the theory of evolution unacceptable. In the pictures, clockwise from lower left, are some of the principle phyla: protozoa (one-celled creatures); platyhelminthes (flatworms); echinodermata (spiny-skinned animals like starfish); arthropoda (including insects); chordata (fish, amphibians, reptiles, birds, and mammals); mollusca (clams, oysters, snails, slugs); annelida (segmented worms); coelenterata (jellyfish and sea anemones); and porifera (sponges).

COURTESY CCM: GENERAL BIOLOGICAL, INC.: CHICAGO

Norman D. Newell, a Columbia University paleontologist, gives another interesting example, the trilobites (see page 59), ancient sea creatures distantly related to the crabs. He points out that they "illustrate very well the phenomenon of the systematic discontinuity [missing links].... Several superfamilies comprising many families appear abruptly near the base of the Lower Cambrian; others are introduced somewhat higher in the Lower Cambrian. Of the ten superfamilies of Lower Cambrian trilobites, not a single ancestor is known."[2]

This, he says, is true of animals and plants in general. "The earliest members of higher categories, phyla, classes, orders, and superfamilies generally have all of the basic characteristics of those categories rather than dominantly ancestral characters. Thus, the higher categories tend to be separated sharply from other related groups with little or no tendency for intergradation.... Many of the discontinuities tend to be more and more emphasized with increased collecting."[3]

George G. Simpson of Harvard University, an authority on fossil mammals, points out that among the thirty-two orders of mammals "the earliest and most primitive known members of every order already have the basic ordinal characters, and in no case is an approximately continuous sequence from one order to another known. In most cases the break is so sharp and the gap so large that the origin of the order is speculative and much disputed.

The absence of transitional types (missing links) is an almost universal phenomenon.

"This regular absence of transitional forms is not confined to mammals, but is an almost universal phenomenon, as has long been noted by paleontologists."[4]

Nevertheless, Simpson and Newell would still interpret the absence of missing links as a lack in the fossil record rather than an indication that the links never existed.

In the British scientific journal *Nature*, the botanist T. G. Tutin describes the absence of connecting links among the major plant groups: "In the ninety-two years since the publication of the *Origin of Species* a great deal of argument but remarkably little fact has been produced about the relationships of the Angiosperms [flowering plants].... Indeed, one may go further and say that no more is known now about the origin of any major groups of plants than was known in 1859."[5]

Fossil horses have changed, but they are horses still.

The fossil record leaves so many unsolved problems that creationists believe that the major groups of living things must have been separately created. Of course, there has been change in the smaller units, the lower categories, but this sort of change is to be expected. There is no clear evidence that minor changes added together have produced new basic types.

There is a series of fossil horses which have undergone change, but they are all horses still. They are adapted for various environments such as marshy terrain and open prairie. Series of fossil ammonites (seashells similar to the chambered nautilus) have also changed somewhat, but they were ammonites all the way through, not something else. The same is true of delicate one-celled animals of the foraminifera group, lamp shells and many others.

Occasionally we find fossils of extinct life forms whose place is between widely separated present-day groups. *Archaeopteryx*, for instance, is a little-known type of

Opposite page: artist's conception of an archaeopteryx, a fossil type with characteristics resembling both birds and reptiles. Archaeopteryx may represent another group, distinct from both types.

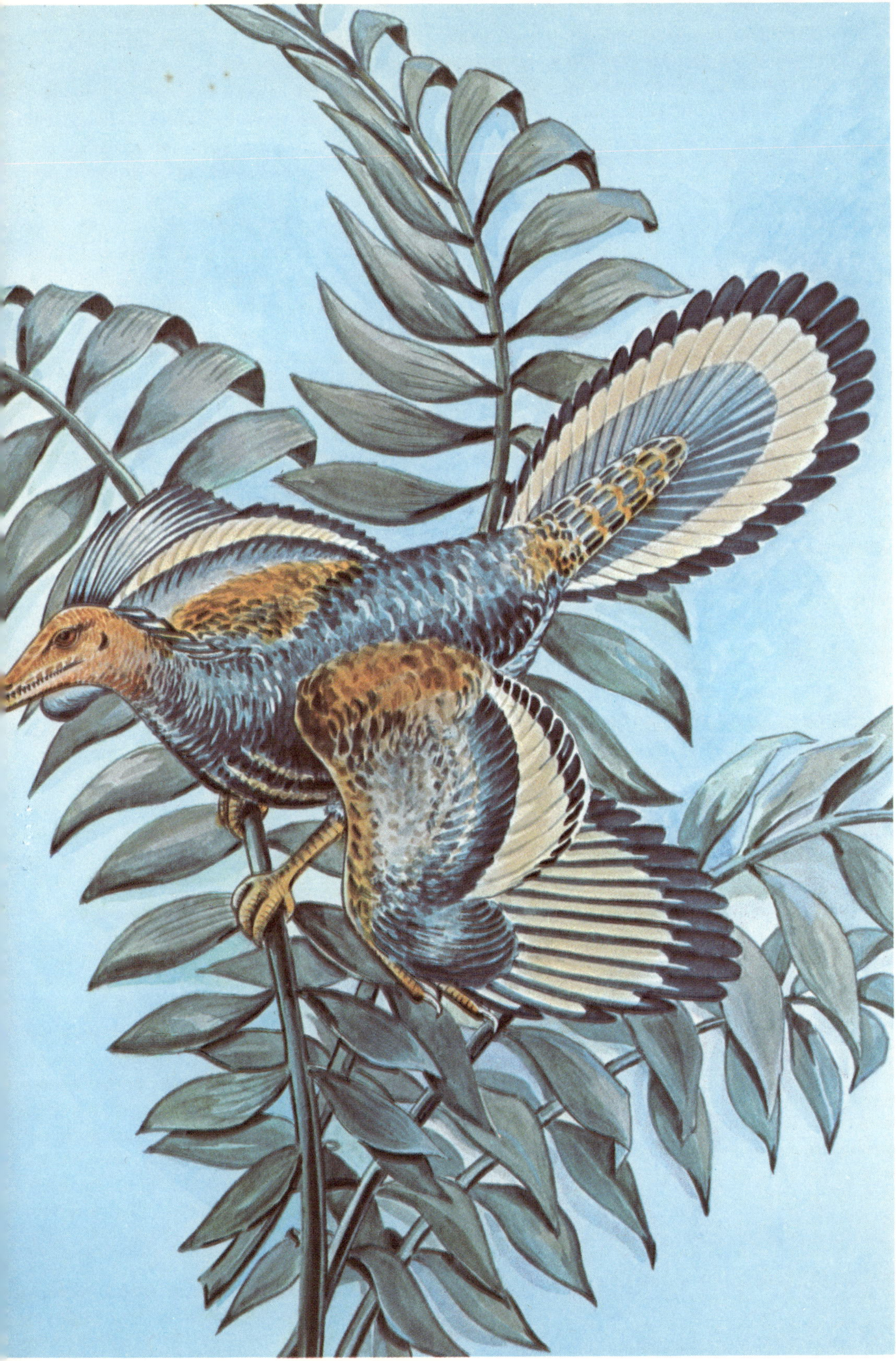

fossil resembling both birds and reptiles. But this may represent another group, distinct from both types. In the fossil record, the higher categories remain separate from the time they first appeared. Those who accept the theory of evolution believe that the fossil record gives the time of origin and evolution of many groups; but this view, like that of missing links, is at best only opinion. If actual transitions are not preserved in the record because of its spotty nature, can we rely on that record in other matters? Can we, for example, be sure that the *lowest* occurrence of a fossil in the earth strata represents the *first* appearance of a plant or animal? The fossil record not only fails to prove organic evolution, but presents serious problems for the theory as well.

Study typical charts picturing supposed evolutionary relationships of animals and plants. Notice how the branches of the animal kingdom connect. In children's science books these charts usually show broad connections. But advanced textbooks show these connections as dotted lines. This is because the evolutionary connections are not supported by fossils; they are only speculative, based on similarities. The large branches in evolutionary "trees" are held together only by theory. To some thoughtful students, these problems make the theory of evolution unacceptable.

Among countless thousands of fossils collected, one might expect a few missing links.

Others have proposed solutions. The most common, as mentioned above, is that the fossil record is not complete. We don't have the missing links simply because we have not found them yet. True, the record *is* spotty and incomplete. But for some environments, such as the deposits under shallow seawaters, the fossil record is "rich beyond the most optimistic prediction." Among the countless thousands of fossils collected from such environments and all over the earth, one might expect to find among those forms consistently preserved as fossils a few "missing links" if they ever existed.

Would blind fate always miss recording missing links between higher categories, yet preserve great numbers of other fossils?

Some have suggested that most major evolutionary changes may have occurred quite rapidly, while the population levels of the respective types were low. This idea may have merit, but is it likely that blind fate would *always miss* recording missing links between higher categories and yet preserve great numbers of fossils of the

Typical "tree of life" diagram from an old textbook misleads the reader. The implied broad connections with the trunk are hypothetical, not proven fact.

Branches of animal life

This diagram is intended to suggest the origin of various animal forms, with the constant progressive departure from ancestral types, now in one direction and now in another, like the branching of a tree. Of course only the main branches are shown.

species or basic types? Also, ought not some intermediate kinds of creatures have been successful enough to survive till today—if they ever did exist? Perhaps the most natural explanation is that the missing links between major groups never existed.

Paleontology contributes little to the solution of basic problems of evolution. Though few realize it, evolution is no more than a working hypothesis.

Contrary to popular opinion, paleontology contributes little to the solution of the basic problems of the theory of evolution. Besides the missing link problem, there is the question of how life originated. British zoologist G. A. Kerkut points out that "it is a matter of faith on the part of the biologist that biogenesis [spontaneous generation of life] did occur, and he can choose whatever method of biogenesis happens to suit him personally; the evidence for what did happen is not available."[6]

Some may be surprised, even distressed, to learn that so much of biological theory rests upon such a shaky foundation. But, as Kerkut points out, the general theory of evolution is no more than a working hypothesis. Neither in the fossil record nor in the living world has it been demonstrated or confirmed.

It is also true that no one can *prove* that the branches of life were divinely created. One must base his beliefs on evaluation of truth from every source. Then one's choice must be made on the weight of evidence, not on demonstration or proof.

Those who are impressed by the failure of paleontology to solve some of the fundamental problems of evolution, and equally impressed by the order and intricacy of living things, may reasonably view the origin and diversity of life as the work of a Creator. If it takes a high degree of intelligence even to understand the phenomena of nature, it may take a much higher degree to design these phenomena.

REFERENCES

1. Austin H. Clark, *The New Evolution: Zoogenesis* (Baltimore: Williams and Wilkins Company, 1930).
2. Norman D. Newell, "The Nature of the Fossil Record," *Proceedings of the American Philosophical Society*, April, 1959, 103(2), pages 264-285.
3. *Ibid.*
4. George G. Simpson, *Tempo and Mode in Evolution* (New York: Columbia University Press, 1944).
5. T. G. Tutin, "Phylogeny of Flowering Plants: Fact or Fiction?" *Nature*, 1952, 126.
6. G. A. Kerkut, *The Implications of Evolution* (New York: Pergamon Press, 1960).

11.
Dimensions of the Mind

When we consider that our deepest understanding of the universe depends upon what is constructed through thought patterns in the brain, we may conclude that the brain is the most complex and self-determining thing in nature.

T. Joe Willey

Each night the sky is set with flecks of fire. We gaze at the glittering configurations overhead and feel almost overwhelmed as we sense the order and dependability of the revolving heavenly vault.

If we wish, we may aid the eye by using a telescope to view the heavens. Then, where we saw only one star, now we see a thousand. From astronomy we have learned that we live on the outskirts of one galaxy among billions of others. We know that the universe is incredibly vast. We get the impression that our understanding of the universe is just beginning to emerge, even though so many mysteries in the heavens have been solved. The prospect of a larger cosmos is even more humbling than before.

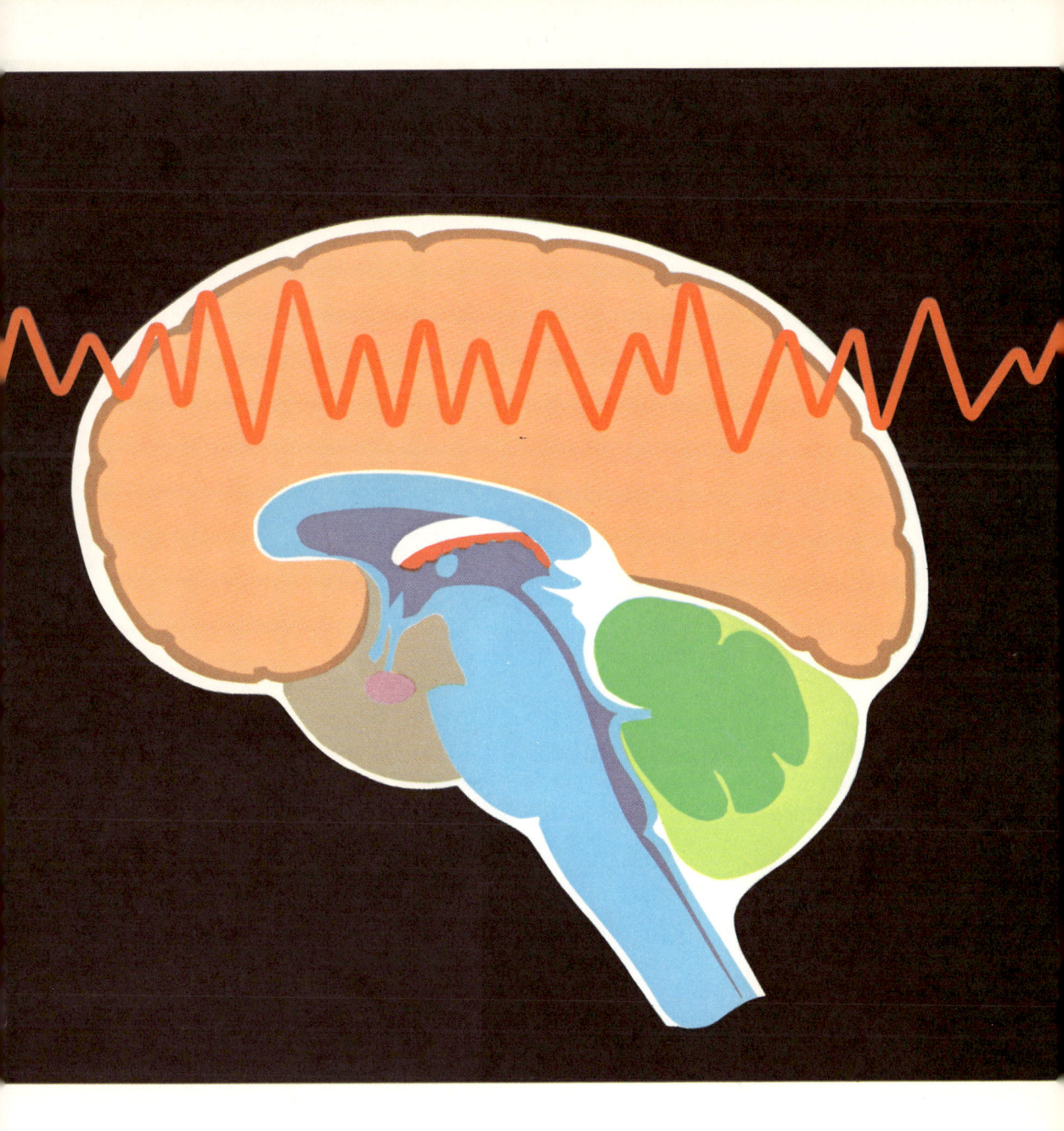

Yet there is something much closer to us that is no less complex than the universe, and hardly as well known. It is the human brain. Even with today's electron microscope, and with advancing technology to explore the brain, we stand only at the door to knowing the enormously complex structure above our shoulders.

The brain has 10 billion or more nerve cells, each of which may be connected to a hundred or more other nerve cells. The possible combination of connecting patterns that could be established is a staggering 2^{100}. Just thinking about such a complex "enchanted loom," over which conscious and unconscious events register, probably invokes a long series of electric impulses in our mind.

But when we consider that our deepest understanding of the universe depends upon what is constructed through thought patterns in the brain, we may conclude that perhaps the brain is the most complex and self-determining thing in all nature.

Ancient Egyptians pulled the brain out with a wire loop and discarded it before mummification.

Ancient Egyptians did not give to the brain the same importance that we do. Attempting to preserve their dead for an afterlife, they unceremoniously pulled the brain out through the nose with a wire loop and discarded it. They considered the heart the primary organ of the body, believing that after death it was weighted against Truth by the god Osiris. But the brain was pitched out onto the sand during mummification.

Some Greeks argued for the heart, some for the brain.

The classical Greeks, to whom we owe so many ideas, were about equally divided over which organ, the heart or the brain, served for the intellect, the passions, and the seat of the soul. The Hippocratic writers believed the brain to be the dominant location where "we think, comprehend, see, and hear, that we distinguish the ugly from the beautiful, the bad from the good." Plato taught that the brain is the supreme organ of the body, assigning thought to it, passions to the heart, and appetites to the belly. But Aristotle argued for the heart as the center of thought and sensation, believing that the brain worked as a refrigerator to cool the heart. At the time the Old Testament was translated into Greek (finished during the second century B.C.), civilized men still considered the heart as the center of understanding.

"Tell me, where is fancy bred, Or in the heart or in the head?"

Four hundred years after Aristotle, Galen (c. A.D. 130–c. 200) argued for the head as the seat of intelligence. He refuted Aristotle: "Why is the brain capable of cooling the heart, and why is the heart not rather capable of heating the brain which is placed above it, since all heat tends to rise? And why does the brain send to the heart only an imperceptible nerve while all the sensory organs draw a large part of their substance from the brain?" Galen, favoring the Hippocratic approach to medicine, learned a great deal of anatomy by dissecting animals. His voluminous writings were regarded as the ultimate authority on anatomy and physiology until William Harvey shook the foundations of medical theory in 1628. Some still regarded the heart as the center of understanding through the seventeenth century. For example, Descartes (1596-1650) wrote that some would put the soul of man in the heart "because the passions are felt in it." And Shakespeare (1564-1616) had Portia sing, "Tell me, where is fancy bred, Or in the heart or in the head?"

Early human anatomy was based on a combination of animal dissection and imagination. Gradually, however, the brain became more important to anatomists. They reasoned that the brain occupied the sum-

The brain has 10 billion or more nerve cells, each of which may be connected to a hundred or more other nerve cells. The possible combination of connecting patterns that could be established is a staggering 2^{100}. Just thinking about such a complex "enchanted loom," over which conscious and unconscious events register, probably invokes a long series of electric impulses in our mind.

mit of the body; it had a spherical form and thus almost a perfect figure; and it was protected by elaborate membranes.

During the Renaissance the lid was lifted above the mystery, and men began again to peer inside the cranial vault. The old speculations about the brain were cast aside or refined as a result of direct observations. Cardiocentric believers were jarred by the discovery that during embryogenesis nerves develop directly from the brain, whereas blood vessels develop independently from the heart.

Even today, some people think of the heart as the center for the emotions, though they know better. One rarely sees a Valentine card showing a brain with an arrow through it! Now, most people know what is meant by the expression, "to pound some sense into your head." And if people still believed the soul of man resided in the heart, they would oppose heart transplants far more than they do.

The brain and the spinal cord, comprising the central nervous system, are well protected.

Three membranes, called meninges, cover the brain. In addition the brain floats in cerebrospinal fluid, which among other things, serves to absorb shocks. Finally a two-layered bony vault, the cranium, provides hard-headed protection. The spinal cord is protected in the same way, but the column of protective vertebrae surrounding the cord is also able to bend. The brain and spinal cord together are considered the central nervous system.

Other nervous elements, such as sense receptors, nerve trunks, and ganglia, outside the central nervous system, are considered the peripheral nervous system, which link the central nervous system with all other parts of the body. These too are protected, usually by being embedded deep in muscles or covered by strong connective tissue.

The brain performs incredibly complicated feats of thinking and memory storage.

All the body's voluntary movements, plus the receiving of stimuli from the eyes, ears, nose, and other sense organs, are controlled through the central nervous system, which simultaneously governs involuntary activities like breathing, metabolism, and heartbeat. The brain also performs incredibly complicated thinking and memory storing. All this is done by that extraordinary "ball of fat" in our heads—the brain —which accounts for only one fiftieth of the body's weight.

The brain, the size and shape of a small pumpkin, weighs about three pounds and feels like unbaked bread dough.

If you were to hold a human brain in your hand, you would discover that it weighs about three pounds and is about the size and shape of a small pumpkin. It feels like unbaked bread dough. Its surface, divided down the middle by a fissure, is extensively folded or convoluted around a brainstem connected to the spinal cord. Behind the main mass of the cerebral cortex is the cerebellum. The outer mantle or gray matter of the cerebral cortex contains layers of nerve cells, called neurons.

Scientists have learned how to chart the functional regions of the brain by applying electric currents to different cerebral parts. (1) visual, (2) weight and form perception, (3) thinking, (4) skin and muscle sensory, (5) trunk, arms, and legs, (6) judgment, (7) speech, (8) mouth and throat, (9) hearing, (10) word understanding. Spaces at the right show relative amounts of brain tissue controlling different parts of the body. (However, there is complex interplay between brain regions, and the brain goes about its business as a unit, not one spot at a time.)

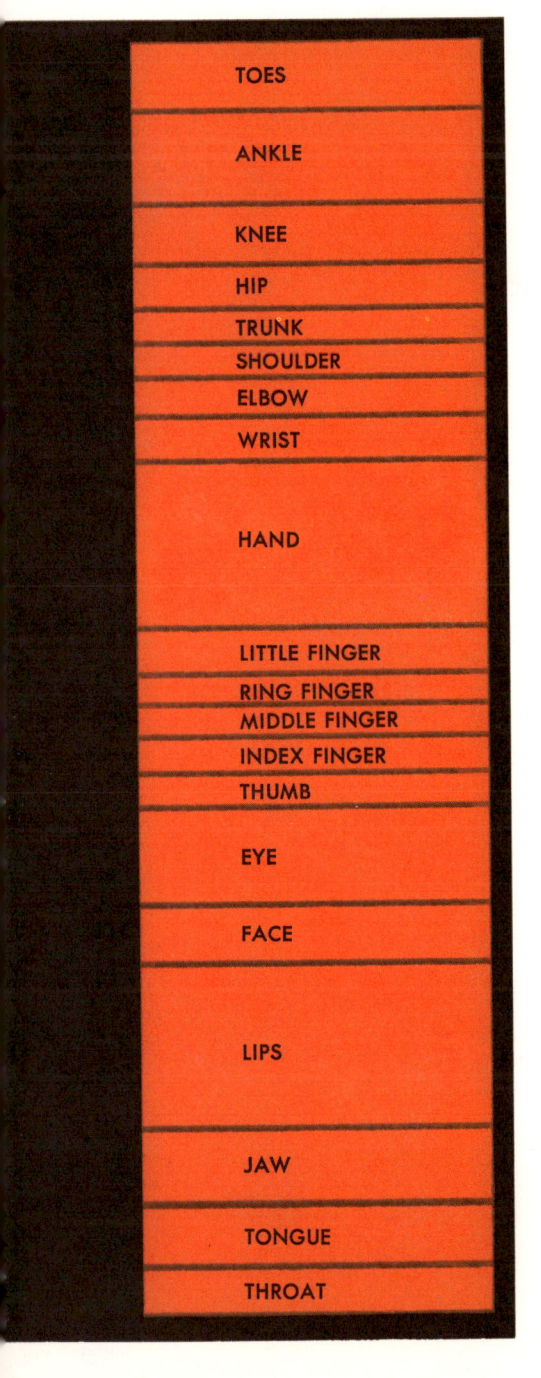

TOES
ANKLE
KNEE
HIP
TRUNK
SHOULDER
ELBOW
WRIST
HAND
LITTLE FINGER
RING FINGER
MIDDLE FINGER
INDEX FINGER
THUMB
EYE
FACE
LIPS
JAW
TONGUE
THROAT

There are also neuroglial cells, which interpose themselves between the neurons and the blood supply to assure that certain chemicals do not enter the brain. Beneath the gray mantle is a white matter of fatty insulated nerve fibers or axons which make connections to all parts of the cerebrum, cerebellum, and spinal cord. A large bundle of fibers also connects the two hemispheres of the divided brain across a bridge called the corpus callosum. Deep inside the brain are ventricles filled with cerebrospinal fluid. When communication between these ventricles and the body outside the brain fails, and excess fluid fills and distends the ventricles, a condition called hydrocephalus ("water on the brain") results.

Important sensory information gained from both inside and outside the body passes through a gateway of nuclei called the thalamus, which lies between the brainstem and the cortex. Part of this information is routed to the hypothalamus just below the thalamus. Here the body's temperature, water balance, and food intake are controlled.

Prompt automatic adjustments of heart, respiration, eyes, skin, stomach, spleen, and the hormones in the blood.

The hypothalamus and thalamus do a lot more than this. When you engage in simple muscular exercise, you get prompt automatic adjustments in heart and respiration rate. More complicated reactions occur when you face an extreme "fight or flight" situation. This involves nearly all body organs. The pupils of your eyes dilate. Blood vessels in your stomach and skin

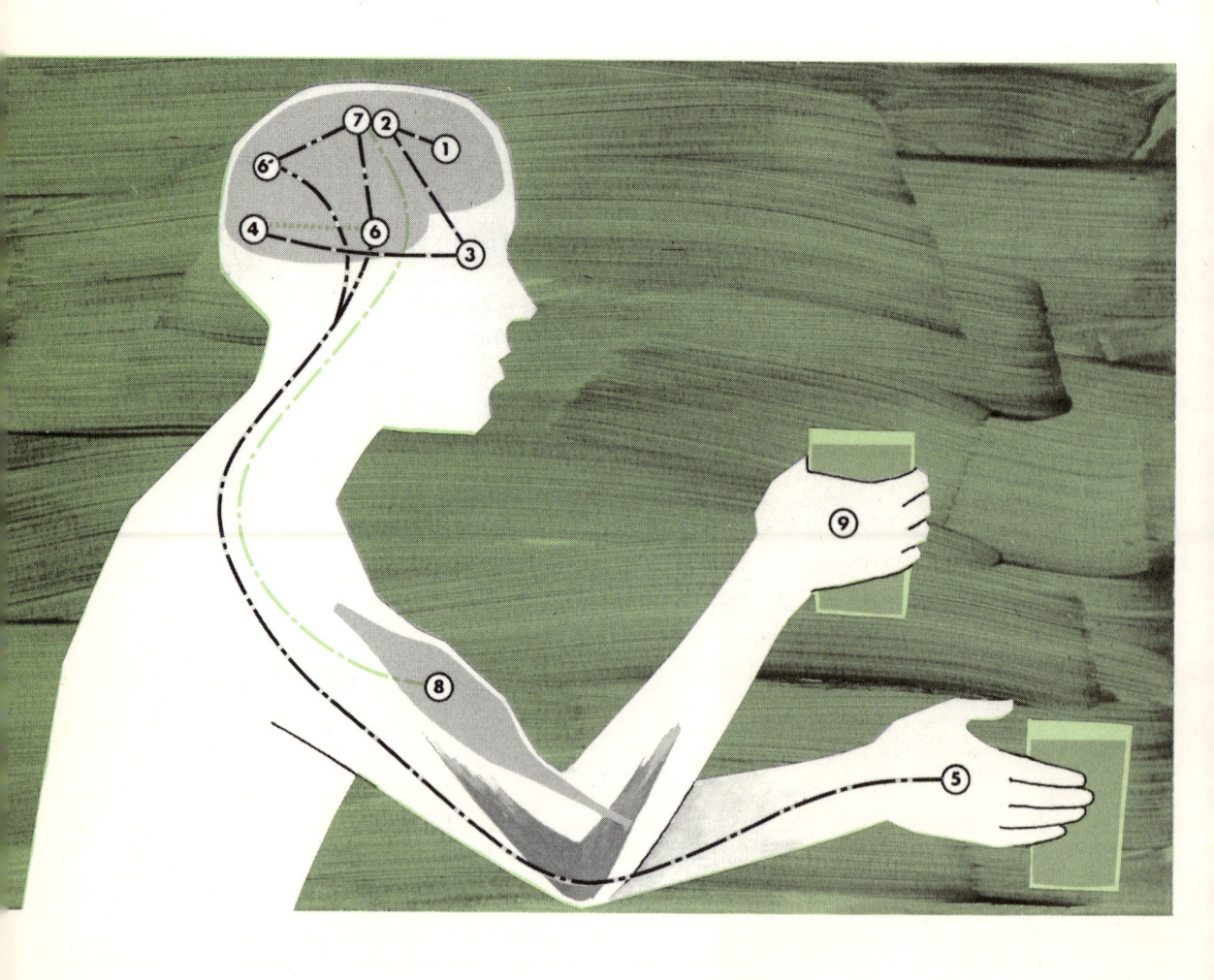

Millions of neurons, located in different parts of the brain, may be involved in a "simple" activity such as taking a drink of water. The illustration, greatly simplified, shows nerve impulses between (1) desire, (2) judgment, (3) eyes, (4) vision, (5) hand, (6 and 6') weight and form perception, (7) reason, (8) motor reflex, and (9) hand.

constrict. Your spleen contracts. Adrenal hormone is released into your bloodstream. Hairs on the back of your neck stand erect. High up in the chain of command a decision is made either to beat a hasty retreat or to stand and fight.

The interplay of conscious sensations with the hypothalamus sometimes leads to psychosomatic diseases. Worry and tensions can cause peptic ulcer and migraine headaches. The nervous system is affected by all we do and nearly everything that goes on about us. We can often detect a lie in someone else because of his involuntary responses such as flushed skin or sweaty hands.

The nose can detect one one hundred trillionth of a pound of garlic odor per quart of air.

Nerve cells normally convey messages in one direction. A sense neuron carries an impulse to the brain or spinal cord, and a different neuron carries motor impulses from the central nervous system to muscles or glands. Sensory neurons, which carry a running commentary to the brain, are extremely sensitive. The nose, for example, can detect .00000000000001 (one one hundred trillionth) of a pound of garlic odor per quart of air. Movements of the tympanum, or eardrum, by less than the diameter of a hydrogen atom (.00000001 cm—one one hundred millionth), are audible. It is still puzzling why vibrations produced by the flow of the blood through the vessels in the ear do not distract hearing. Receptors in the eye sense radiation almost as little as one light quantum, the smallest unit of radiant energy. An estimated 3 to 4 million sensing devices in the skin report to the brain changes of pressure and temperature. During waking periods the brain nonchalantly accepts heavy bombardments of background noise from sensory organs and treats it as trivial, unless a particular sensation is novel or harmful. When instant action is called for, as when one accidently touches a hot stove, the impulse commanding removal of the hand bypasses the brain. Instead, it goes through the spinal cord and over motor fibers to the muscles. This hand-removing command may travel 250 miles per hour. Following the short delay for processing the command, the hand is removed almost immediately, and the sharp perception of the burning hand is not detected until slightly later. In other words, the hand is removed before further burning takes place while the brain decides what to do!

Electrochemical signals scurry over nerve networks; as many as 1,000 impulses a second can be conveyed over a nerve.

All sensory receptors convert their stimuli into tiny electrochemical signals. These signals scurry over nerve networks by an ingenious operation. Positive sodium ions surround the nerve and enter only for a short time during impulse signalling. Relative to the outside, the inside of the nerve is usually kept negative. But when sodium is temporarily admitted, the inside of the nerve turns positive. This touches off a whole series of changes on down the line of the nerve, with adjacent sodium ions moving in and potassium ions being kicked out. The switching of ions may go on so

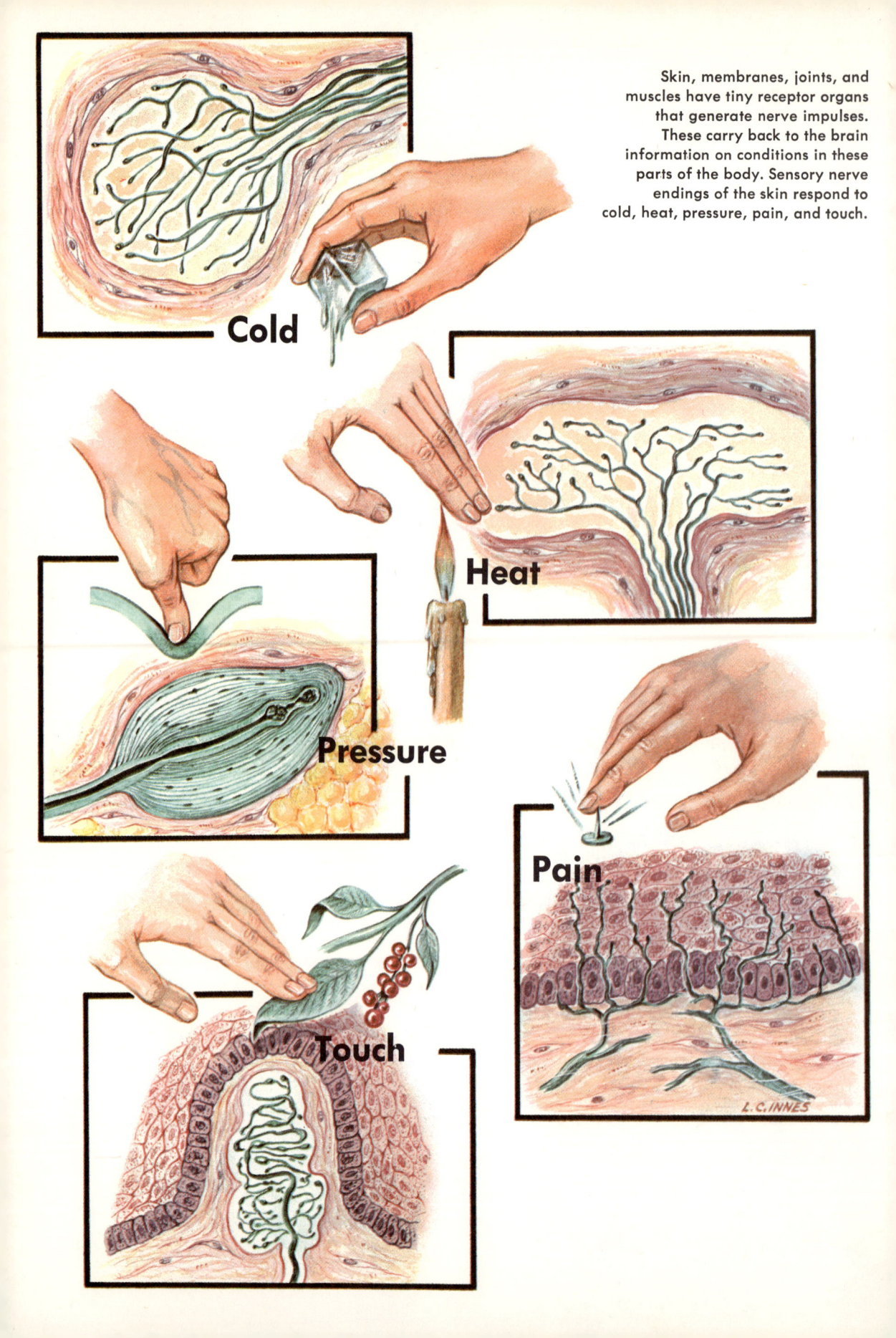

Skin, membranes, joints, and muscles have tiny receptor organs that generate nerve impulses. These carry back to the brain information on conditions in these parts of the body. Sensory nerve endings of the skin respond to cold, heat, pressure, pain, and touch.

Cold

Heat

Pressure

Pain

Touch

fast that 1,000 impulses per second can be conveyed over a nerve. The axon ends in a bag containing small packets of chemicals. These are thought to contain a transmitter substance which is ejected across a minute gap (synapse) between an axon and a dendrite. This action initiates electrochemical events on the dendritic side and the impulse continues on its way. Without a chemical relay the impulse would stop dead.

"Brain waves" are not easy to interpret.

In 1924 Hans Berger pasted metal strips to his son's scalp and recorded irregular electrical activity which, he thought, apparently came from brain operations below the skull. He called them "brain waves." Five years later, following publication of his observation, people speculated that the wiggles contained detailed information about the mental processes in the brain. That was a bit optimistic! Nonetheless, the electroencephalograph (EEG) is used in various ways to analyze normal and damaged brains. What the EEG actually records from the scalp is an average of what is going on in large populations of neurons. So little is understood that the job of sorting out any meaning from the wobbly lines is enormous. The situation is akin to being in the center of a large convention hall where people are chattering in small groups and attempting to hear all the conversations at once. Electrodes placed on the scalp pick up discharging neuron activity from cells surrounding the electrode and

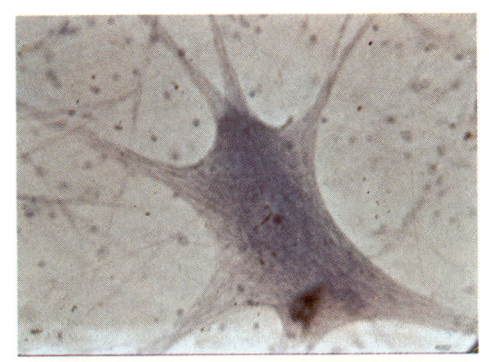

Top: nerve cell, from spinal cord smear.
Middle: human nerve fibers.
Below: cells of spinal ganglion.

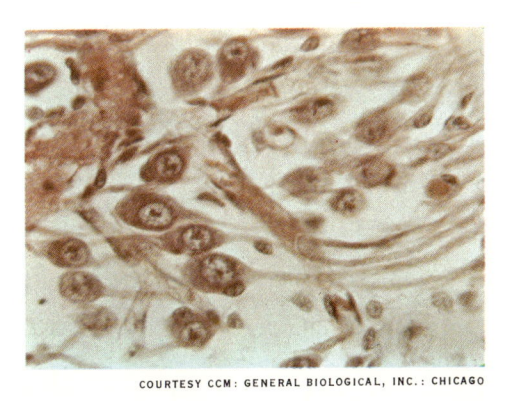

COURTESY CCM: GENERAL BIOLOGICAL, INC.: CHICAGO

amplify them several thousand times. Even the brightest idea cannot generate enough voltage to light one neon tube. In fact, it has been estimated that 60,000 scalps might provide enough energy to operate a flashlight.

Since early times people have tried to localize the seat of the soul, and mental functions, in certain areas of the brain. Colorful and enormously popular during the early nineteenth century was Gall's cranioscopy or phrenology, the practice of trying to read a man's character and personality by feeling the bumps on his skull.

Many physiologists, to whom this idea seemed ridiculous, tried to discredit Gall's speculations by damaging portions of animals' brains and studying the results. They also observed human patients with brain defects. As knowledge of brain function grew, phrenology declined.

The frontal cortex—important area for the personality of the individual.

Scientists learned how to chart the functional regions of the brain by applying electrical currents to different cerebral parts.

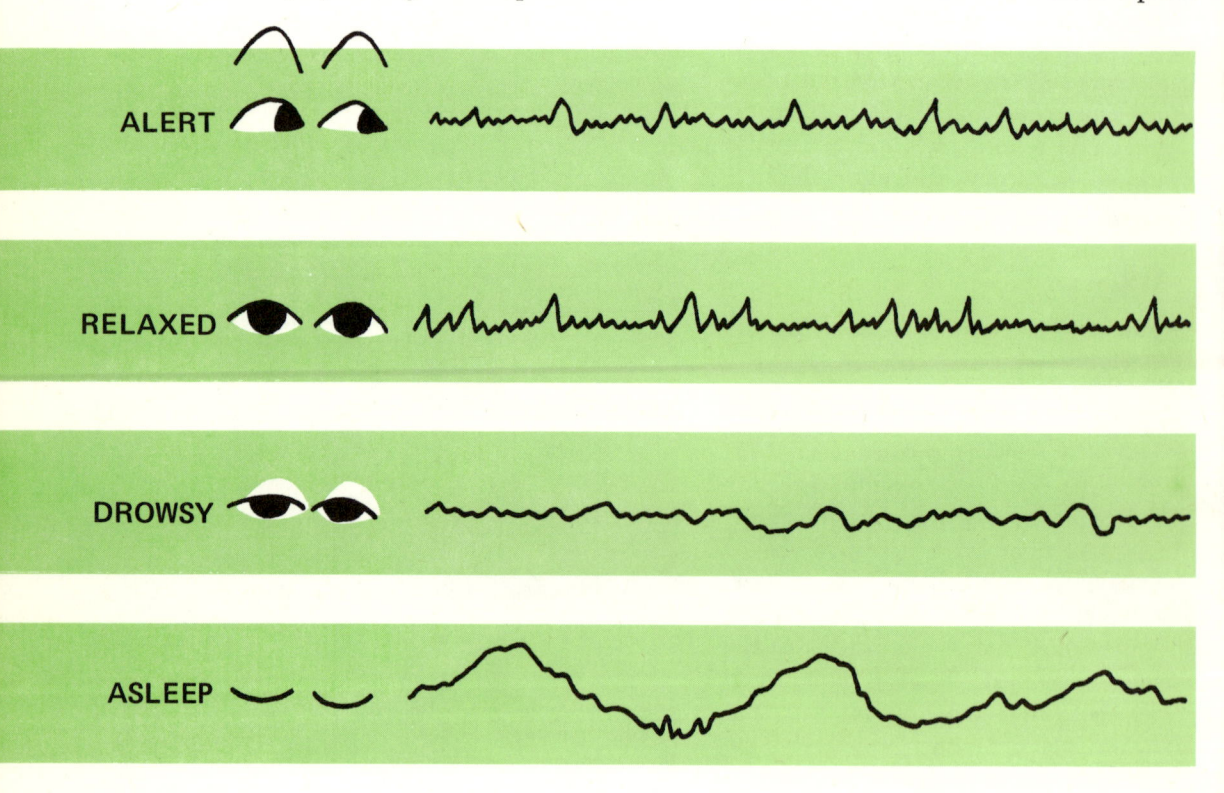

ALERT

RELAXED

DROWSY

ASLEEP

The electroencephalograph (EEG) can only record the average of what is going on in large populations of neurons. It cannot easily sort out specific meanings. However, there is a definite correlation between the EEG recording and various states of mental alertness. The alert mind gives a sharp pattern, and as mental alertness declines, the sharp peaks flatten into undulating waves, resembling ocean breakers.

They learned that the vision sensory area was located in the back of the brain, speech along the side, voluntary motor control in a strip of cortex in front of another region concerned with body senses. The frontal cortex was found to be "silent," producing no overt response to electrical stimulations. Damage to this area in an adult did not impair physical processes of the body; rather it produced a lack of drive to organize thoughts and actions, and it released previous inhibitions. This discovery tended to establish this area as important for the personality of an individual.

Neurosurgeons, while exploring other areas during electrical stimulations of the brain, sometimes brought memories of previous events back into consciousness. A past experience or a Christmas song held in memory since early childhood might be replayed by applying electrical currents through an electrode.

When some other regions were stimulated with electric currents, these produced sensations of pleasure or pain. During pleasurable stimulation, the patient often requested more, while during painful stimulation the patient begged for the current to be turned off. All of these experiments seemed to establish that specific parts of the brain took care of specific functions.

Attempting to divide the brain into specific individual units of activity, however, is naïve. Experimenters used to think that parcels of cortex performed independently of one another. Now we know this is only partly true. There is a complex interplay of different activities between brain regions. The brain goes about its business as a unit despite the artificial way we may look at it. A simple activity, such as deciding how to spend a nickel in a candy shop or pinning a tail on a donkey blindfolded, is not cared for by just one spot or region in the brain.

Disassembly of the elements that make up a structure such as the brain is a closely followed doctrine in the neurosciences as in all sciences. Near complete acceptance of reductionism, the procedure of reducing complex phenomena to simple terms, is widespread. Holism, a theory that in nature a whole cannot be reduced into the sum of its parts, is seen as neither respectable nor useful. There is no question that the breaking up the whole into its parts has produced an avalanche of knowledge. But is it possible to reconstruct the sum of the parts and retrieve the information lost during the process of reducing the whole? According to information theory, the answer is No! Yet distrust of the phrase, "The whole is more than the sum of its parts," is evident today in the setting up of many scientific experiments.

The brain is not a machine and cannot be explained as such.

Reductionism tends to lead one into oversimplified statements about nature. The extravagant claim that the computer performs like a human brain and is consequently threatening to replace man provides a ready example. The input to a computer is compared to the sensory code to the brain,

Rabbit

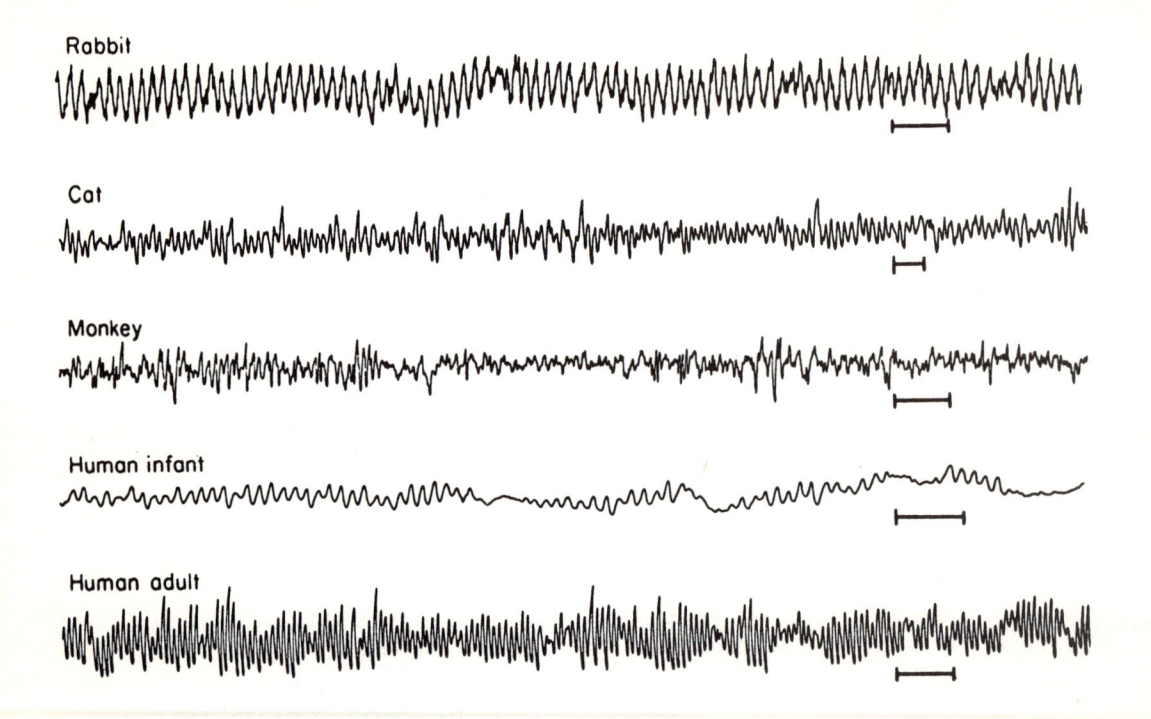

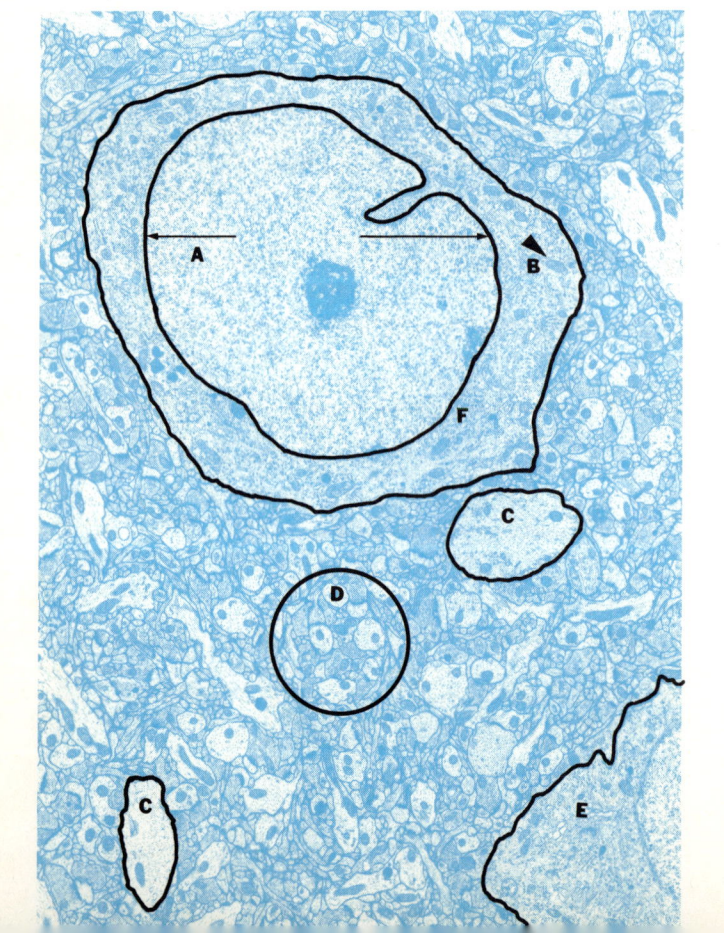

Cat

Monkey

Human infant

Human adult

Above: electroencephalogram (EEG) tracings from various species. These tracings show variations in electrical energy generated by activity in brain cells. The calibration bar below each tracing equals one second.

Opposite page: This electron micrograph pictures structure of a rat's visual cortex. Smaller picture at left gives the key for identifying areas indicated by letters.

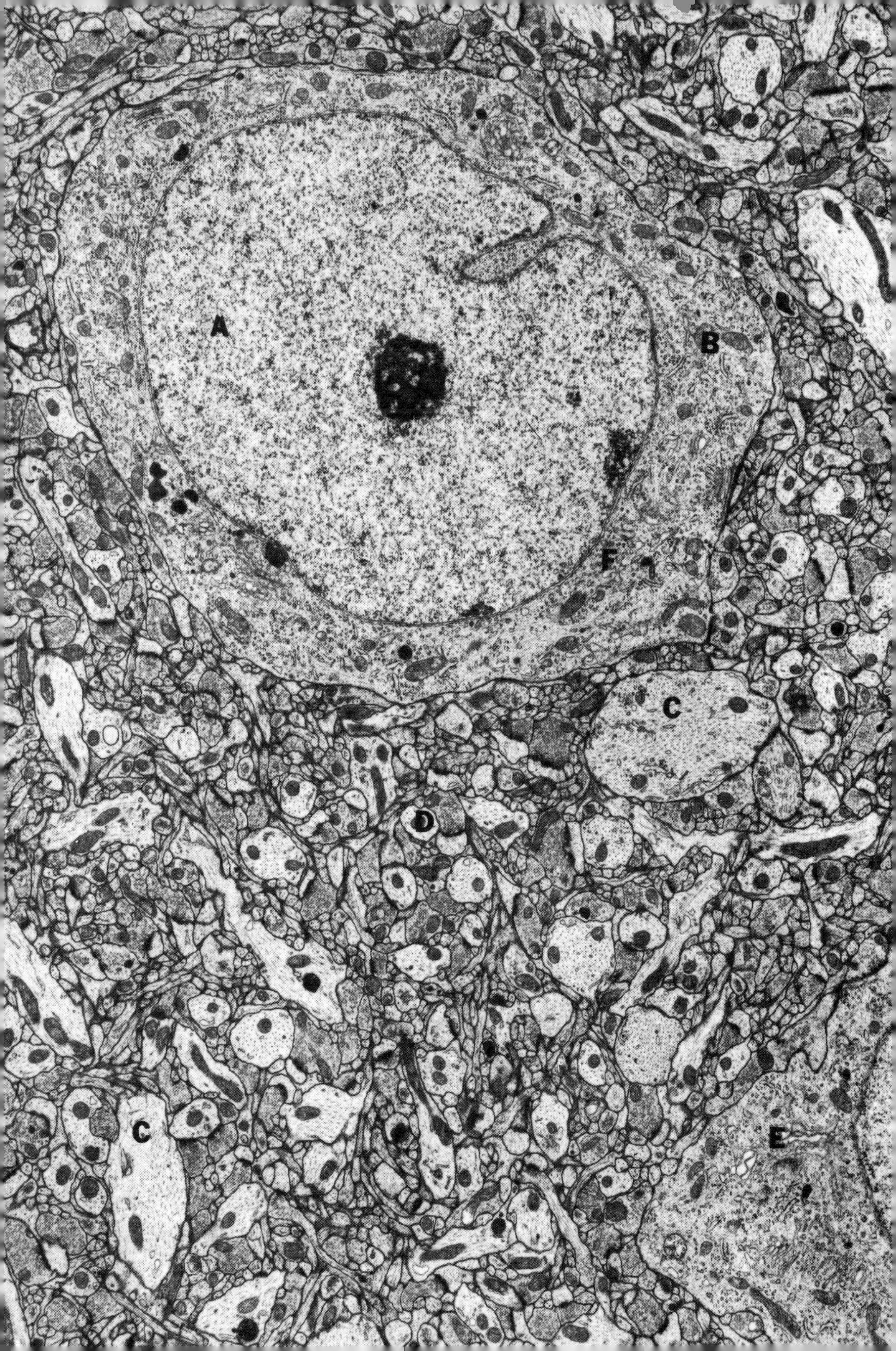
A
B
F
C
D
C
E

Even the brightest idea cannot generate enough voltage to light one neon tube.... An estimated ... 60,000 scalps might provide enough energy to operate a flashlight.

and the brain output is specified as behavior. But the comparison fails; no one really understands what goes on in the brain in processing the sensory inflow and in deciding upon the mode of behavior. We do know, however, that the brain does *not* reach its decisions by the mechanical logic that we understand for the computer. Furthermore, the human brain is not a machine and cannot be explained as one, even though the meaning of "machine" has changed with technological advances.

Descartes: Man is as automated as the heavens, though man has a soul, a tiny flicker, not part of the machine.

Mechanistic physiology, explaining function of the body in terms of a machine, can be traced back to Descartes. He theorized that function was explicable only in terms of the machine. To avoid Galileo's fate, Descartes modestly confined his treatise to his desk, where it remained unpublished until after his death. Descartes reasoned that the human body is a machine. The action of digestion, the beating of the pulse, and the functioning of the five senses can be explained by physical laws just as mechanics explain star movements. Man, he said, is as automated as the heavens. Assuming that God created matter and endowed the world with laws to govern it, Descartes was faced with the problem of making man different from a star. So he said that man has a soul through which God mysteriously arranges the interaction of body and mind. The soul, said Descartes, a tiny flicker, not part of the machine, has its seat in the pineal gland, in the middle of the brain. Control over motion and sensation occurs by the opening and closing of valves in the brain, as a pipe organ is controlled by pedals and keys. There is no allowance for the soul to intervene in reflex action. This machine goes about its business like a well-oiled clock.

"I repeat," Descartes wrote, "I want you to regard these functions as taking place naturally in this machine because of the very arrangements of its parts, neither more nor less than do the movements of a clock or other automaton from the weights and wheels, so that there is no need on their account to suppose in it any soul vegetative or sensitive or any principle of life other than its blood."

Thus Descartes envisioned a dualism between mind and body. The influence of his thinking is still alive today, though recent scientific discoveries have shown it to be defective. Many body functions can, of course, be explained in mechanical terms. Digestion operates by chemical laws. Movements of the head to watch a bird in flight can be understood using systems theory. Breathing and circulation, though complicated and still not fully understood, are governed by physical laws. Blood passes through the body by the physical pumping action of the heart and by osmotic forces. We now possess more knowledge about "mechanical man" than Descartes could have imagined. We know that physical laws *do* precisely regulate the body. However, as our understanding of nature increases, we can also see that man is more than just a physical machine. This fact should make us more sensitive to the dignity of life and the nature of man.

Thanks to the assumption that the body is mechanistic, operating by the laws of physics and chemistry, we have a vast amount of knowledge about the body. But trying to dismember the mind and formulate its operation as a mere mechanism has not been as fruitful. Naturalism, in its limited area, has proved enormously successful in solving problems. But trying to apply it to all things is almost like saying: "If an aspirin is good for headaches, it is also good for the plague." Thwarted by efforts to observe the mind through skillfully designed experiments, some scientists have decided that either consciousness is an epiphenomenon, or the problem is hopeless. In spite of this, few individuals deny an awareness of feeling, thinking, perceiving, and willing, all of which are experienced through the conscious mind.

Dualism retards a proper conception of man.

Dualism—separating man into body and mind—is workable in some areas of science. But this approach retards a proper conception of man. On the one hand, rigorous mechanistic science has successfully given us acceptable answers to many former questions. Science has promoted our health and social welfare and helped us control natural events and resources. We have convincing evidence of mechanisms in function. Consequently, man tends to regard himself as a machine, and indeed, body function can be explained reasonably well this way.

The transformation of man's thinking

so that he regards himself as a machine, his behavior as mechanical, and his brain as a computer, has also been aided by deterministic psychology. Philosophical determinism is based on a physical theory that describes a system when one knows precisely the state of the system at any given instant. Laplace (1749-1827), a French mathematician, applied Newton's theory of gravitation to celestial mechanics, attempting to prove the solar system to be strictly mechanical. Later in life Laplace extended the same scheme to psychology and supported Magendie's physiological determinism. During the eighteenth and nineteenth centuries determinism was a dominant philosophy in physics, though it had been criticized on the ground that experimental evidence was not conclusive.

In 1927 this classical theory was disturbed by Heisenberg's indeterminancy (or uncertainty) principle. According to Heinsenberg it is impossible to fix simultaneously, precisely, both position and momentum of a single particle. The optimistic Laplace wrote that a single formula for large bodies would also work for the lightest atoms. But work in atomic physics began to break this idea down. The act of obtaining the necessary physical information about a particle would so alter its characteristics that its exact position and momentum would be indeterminable. The recognition of this principle upset the entire philosophical world. And in neurophysiology we see the same principle of uncertainty.

Many psychologists today still attempt to explain man's behavior under the spell of a psychological determinism. This implies that our sense of purpose and our will to decide freely are illusions. Deterministic psychology, an oversimplified method of looking at behavior, gives man a feeling that he is not accountable for his acts. Consequently life seems meaningless; man is an automaton.

Ten million neurons involved in an act of willing?

Scientifically, it is presently impossible to discover whether or not determinism is an operational reality in the mind of man. How would we go about finding out? Would we try to observe the neurons in the brain before and after a particular act of willing? Perhaps 10 million neurons would be involved in that act. Where would one look in the brain? What would one look for? A change in potential? A biochemical alteration during translation from the memory (if memory is stored in chemical code) into action? How much would it disturb the system to observe it? The answer is obvious: It is premature if not impossible to say that the behavior of man is deterministic.

Each of us possesses on his own shoulders a blazing sun to explore the universe, to look at the stars in the heavens and earthworms in his own backyard; to ponder the complexity and order in all of nature. We understand enough about the human brain to know of its impressive order and complexity. It does not function like a simple clock, switchboard, or computer. Through the mind, our most creative element, we can consciously will to pattern our most complex forms of behavior. Practically speaking we know very little about how the mind operates. What we do know should bring us closer to the Creator.

A study of the properties of the mind, the way the brain is put together, and what it can do, can give us a real trust in the creative performance of our Creator. The existence of the human brain can, in fact, be one of the strongest evidences that there is a Creator. For the God who made us gave us minds to appreciate His creatures and designs in nature and to fit us to ponder what He made.

Each of us possesses on his own shoulders a blazing sun to explore the universe, to look at the stars in the heavens and earthworms in his own backyard. . . . The way the brain is put together, and what it can do, can give us a real trust in the creative performance of our Creator.

Contributors

ROBERT E. D. CLARK, *Organic Chemistry*. Ph.D., Cambridge University; honors scholar at St. John's College, Cambridge University; author of *Darwin: Before and After, Christian Belief and Science, The Universe: Plan or Accident?* and *The Christian Stake in Science;* member Cambridge Philosophical Society, Council of Victoria Institute; lecturer in chemistry at Cambridgeshire College of Arts and Technology.

HAROLD G. COFFIN, *Marine Invertebrate Zoology*. Ph.D., University of Southern California; author of *Creation: Accident or Design?* member Sigma Xi, Geological Society of America; chairman Department of Biology, Walla Walla College (Washington), 1956-64; Geoscience Research Institute since 1964.

LLOYD E. DOWNS, *Zoology*. Ph.D., University of Southern California; member Society of Protozoology, Sigma Xi, American Society of Naturalists; Department of Biology, Loma Linda University (La Sierra Campus, California), since 1944; head of department since 1954.

LEONARD N. HARE, *Plant Physiology and Botany*. Ph.D., University of Maryland; since 1961, Department of Biology, Andrews University (Michigan).

ERIC A. MAGNUSSON, *Quantum Chemistry, Inorganic Chemistry*. Ph.D., London University, Ph.D., University of New South Wales; postdoctoral study, Indiana University; fellow London Chemical Society; member Faraday Society; Italian Government visiting scientist award, 1968; professor, Avondale College (Australia).

RICHARD M. RITLAND, *Biology (Paleontology)*. Ph.D., Harvard University; member Sigma Xi, American Association of Anatomists, Society of Vertebrate Paleontology; fellow Geological Society of London, New York Academy of Science; author of *A Search for Meaning in Nature;* formerly assistant professor of anatomy, Loma Linda University, California; professor of paleontology, Andrews University, Michigan.

JOAN BELTZ ROBERTS, *Zoology*. Ph.D., Oregon State University; member Cooper Ornithological Society; Department of Biology, Andrews University (Michigan), 1963-67; missionary in Africa since 1967.

ASA C. THORESEN, *Zoology*. Ph.D., University of Oregon; member American Ornithological Union, Cooper Ornithological Society; chairman Department of Biology, Andrews University (Michigan), since 1963.

JAMES R. VAN HISE, *Physical Chemistry*. Ph.D., University of Illinois; research associate, Oakridge National Laboratory, Argon National Laboratory; visiting lecturer, University of Illinois, Michigan State University; member American Physical Society, American Chemical Society, Phi Lambda Upsilon; author of articles in various scientific journals; chairman Department of Physics, Tri-State College (Indiana).

T. JOE WILLEY, *Physiology*. Ph.D., University of California, Berkeley; member Sigma Xi, American Society for Cell Biology; author of articles on neurophysiology; Loma Linda University School of Medicine, Department of Pharmacology (California).

Credits

Page 2 (1) American Museum of Natural History
(2) Georg Schützenhofer Bild
Page 3 D. Tank
Page 7 Fabian Bachrach, New York
Pages 8, 9 H. Armstrong Roberts
Page 10 D. Tank
Page 12 H. Larkin, artist
Page 13 Asa Thoresen
Page 14 Above, H. Larkin, artist
Below, UPI Photo
Page 15 H. Larkin, artist
Page 16 H. Larkin, artist
Page 17 Above, Walter Scheithauer
Below, H. Larkin
Page 18 (owl) Photo Researchers, Inc.
(chickadee) Henry B. Kane
Pages 20, 21 H. Armstrong Roberts
Page 22 Georg Schützenhofer Bild
Page 23 Bettmann Archive
Pages 24, 27, 28, 29, 30, 31, 32, 35, 37 Courtesy CCM: General Biological, Inc.: Chicago
Pages 38-40 H. Larkin, artist
Page 43 Sven Raven
Page 44 H. Larkin, artist
Page 46 Courtesy CCM: General Biological, Inc.: Chicago
Page 47 Sven Raven
Page 50 D. Tank

Pages 52, 53, 55 H. Larkin, artist
Page 57 (machine) Harold M. Lambert
(potter) Soibelman Syndicate
(builders) Harold M. Lambert
(snow flowers) H. D. Wheeler
Page 58 D. Tank
Page 64 H. Larkin, artist
Pages 66, 69 D. Tank
Pages 70, 71 Loma Linda University
Pages 72, 73 Courtesy CCM: General Biological, Inc.: Chicago
Page 77 H. Armstrong Roberts
Page 80 © San Bernardino County Museum Association. Used by permission.
Page 83 H. Larkin, artist
Page 85 (top to bottom) Courtesy Sylvania Electric Products; A. Devaney, Inc., N.Y.; Samuel Myslis
Page 88 (bobcat) Ed Cesar
Pages 90, 91 H. Larkin, artist
Pages 94, 95 © San Bernardino County Museum Association, by John D. Olmsted
Pages 98, 99 Oran and Bonnie Jean McNiel
Pages 102, 103 H. Larkin, artist
Page 106 Oran and Bonnie Jean McNiel
Page 108 Philip D. Gendreau, N.Y.; Harold Wagar; Robert H. Wright; D. Tank; Ernest Booth
Pages 110, 111 (Top) Richard H. Utt; (others) Courtesy CCM: General Biological, Inc.: Chicago
Pages 113, 114 American Museum of Natural History
Pages 116, 117, 120-122 H. Larkin, artist
Page 124 Lucille Innes
Page 125 Courtesy CCM: General Biological, Inc.: Chicago
Page 126 H. Larkin, artist
Pages 128, 129 Courtesy of Dr. Robert L. Schultz

Index

Italic numbers indicate illustrations.

Adenine 71
Adrenal hormone 123
Aerodynamic design of birds 10
Aileron, birds' 13
Airplanes compared with birds 10, *14, 22, 23*
Air sacs, system of, in birds' bones 10
Albatross 15
Algae 34, *35*
Alula 13, *14*
Amino acids 68-76, *69*, 82, 92, 93
Amoeba 32, 33, 37
Anemone, sea *106*
Angstrom units 101
Arcella 37
Archaeologist 75
Archaeopteryx 112, *113*
Aristotle, on brain 118
Arthropoda 59, 62
Astronomy 102-104
ATP 28
Automation 67, 87
Axelrod, Dr. D. I., quoted 61, 62

Bacteria 34, 68, 79
Barbs 12, *12*
Barbules 12, *12*
Belkengren, Dr. Richard 25
Berger, Hans 125
Bible 56
   quoted 19, 79, 105
Bird, man-o'-war 10
Birds 8-23, 109
Birds', aerodynamic design 10
  blood supply 11
  bones 10, *10*
  brain 15
  breast muscles, 9, 11
  circulation 10
  eyes 11, *11*

feathers 10-15, *12, 13*
flight 12-22, *14-18, 22*
skeleton 10
skull 10
temperature 10
wings 10-19, *12, 14*
Blood cells *70, 71*
Blood pressure, birds' 11
Blue-green algae 34, *35*, 40
Bobcats *80*
Body temperature, birds' 10
Boltzmann 49
Bones, birds' 10
Brachiopods 61, *63, 64*
Brain 116-133, *117, 120, 121, 122, 126*
   ancient ideas on 118, 119
   appearance of 119
   covering of 119
   human 116-133
   waves 125
   weight of 119
Breast muscles, birds' 9, 10
Buzzards 16, *16*

Cambrian fossils 59-65, 112
   abrupt appearance of 61, 112
   discovery of 60
Cambrian, Lower 112
   Middle 59
Canada geese *14*
Carbon 100, 101
Carbon dioxide used in photosynthesis 45
Cat, species of 108
Catalysts, organic 68
Cell 24-37
   generalized *24*
   origin of 26, 36, 37
Cell parts *27, 28*
Cellular "drinking" 27
Ceratium *37*

Cerebellum 119, 121
Cerebrospinal fluid 119
Chemical evolution 75
Chickadee *18*
Chlorophyll 41, 44, 45, *46, 47*, 101, 102
Chloroplast 44
Chloroplastids 41
Chromatin 30
Chromosomes 29, *31*, 89, 93, 94
Cilia 33
Circulation, birds' 10
Clark, A. H., quoted 109
Classification of living things 107-109
Coal, amount of, to produce energy captured by plants 38, 39, *39*
Codons 71
Coelenterates 62
Coleus 41, *42*
Control systems 88-94, *90, 91*
Coral *106*
Corn leaf, cross section of *46*
Cortex, frontal 126, *127*
Crab nebula *96, 104*
Creativity 56, *57*
Creator 19, 37, 56, 65, 79, 105, 115, 132, 133
Crinoids *64*
Crustaceans 59
Crystals *50*
   in liquid *51*
Cytoplasm 30, *31*
Cytosine 71

Daedalus 8
Darwin, Charles 54, 55, 61-64, 82
David, King 19
Death Valley 38
Deoxyribonucleic acid (*see* DNA)
Deoxyribotides 30

De Saussure 40
Descartes 118, 130, 131
Design 87
   argument from 84
Designer 19, 87, 94, 100, 104, 105
Determinism 132
Diatoms 32
Didinium *29*, 33, 34
Difflugia 37
Digestion, birds' efficient 10
Digestive enzymes 68
Dipeptides 68, *69*
Discontinuity 112
DNA 30, 31, 36, 71-78, *72*
Dog and fly, size of, compared 55, *55*
Drosophila, chromosomes in cell of 31
Dualism 131
Ducks *20, 21*
Du Nouy, LeComte, quoted 100

Eagles 16
Echinoids 62
EEG (electroencephalograph) 125, *126*
Egg 30
Egyptian, ancient, and brain 118
Electrochemical signals 123
Elodea canadensis 41

Emerson 45
Emerson effect 45
Endoplasmic reticulum 27
Energy, of universe 52
   radiant 101, *102*
   solar 38-45, 102, *102*
Energy sink 41-45, *44*
Engineer 79
Englemann 40
Entropy 49
Enzymes 34, 68-79, 82, 83, 88-94
Ephelota 37

ER (endoplasmic reticulum) 27
Escherichia coli 68
Eucalyptus leaf, cross section of *46*
Euglena 37
Euplotes 32
Evolutionary theory 55, 64, 65, 79, 82, 115
Evolutionary tree *110,111, 114,*
"Explosive" evolution 64, 65
Eyes, birds' compared with men's 11, *11*
   construction of birds' 11

Factory, cell compared to 37
Families of living things 108, 109
Feathers, construction of 11, 12, *12*, 13
   functions of, in flight 13
Felis 108
"Fight or flight" situation 121
Fish *108,* 109
Flagella 34
Flight, characteristics of, differ 15
   mechanics of birds' 13-22, *14-18,* 22
Fly and dog, size of, compared 55, *55*
Flying machines 23
Flying men, myth of 8, 9
Food made by photosynthesis 45
Fossils 58-65, *62, 63,* 107ff
   Cambrian 64
Foundation, shaky, of evolution 115
Foveae 11

Galaxy *48, 49,* 104
Galen, quoted 118
Galileo 84, 99
Genera 108
Genes 74, 83, 89-92
Gliding flight 15, *15,* 16
Glucose *91,* 92
Glutamine 93
Golden plover 10

Golgi bodies 28, 29
Grana 44
Grand Canyon, worm burrows in 60
Graptolite 62
Gray, Professor 56
Greece, philosophers of 39, 40, 118
Green, why leaves are 40, 41
Greenewalt, Crawford H., on hummingbirds 19
Guanine 71
Guillemots 13, 16
Gulls 8, 9, 16

Hamuli 12, *12*
Harvey, William 118
Hawks 11, 16
Heart vs. head 118, 119
Heisenberg's indeterminacy principle 132
Helicopter, hummingbirds' flight compared to 16, *17*
Hemoglobin 68-71, *70, 71*
Hen, feathers of 11

Hippocratic belief on brain 118
Histidine 92
Holism 127
Hooks (hamuli) 12, *12*
Hormone, adrenal 123
  insulin 68
Horses, fossil 112
Housefly 55
Human Destiny, LeCompte du Nouy's 100
Hummingbirds 11, *17*, 19
Huxley, Julian, quoted 107
Hypothalamus 121

Icarus 8
Indeterminancy principle 132
Ingen-Housz 40

Insulin 68
Intergrana 44

Jellyfish 59, 61, *64*

Katydid 95
Kerkut, G. A., quoted 115
Kingdoms, animals and plant, divisions of 108

Labyrinth 8
Lactose 89-92, *90, 91*
Lamella in leaves 44, 45
Lamp shells 61
Laplace 132
Lederberg, Joshua 36, 78
Leucine 92
Life: How did it happen? 52, 54
Life, tree of 107, *110, 111, 114*
Light 40-45, 101-105
Linnaeus 107
Lizard 95, *108*
Lockyer, Norman 104
Lynx 86

Magic 51, 56
Magnification 97
Man-o'-war bird 10
Mechanistic evolution 75, 79
Mechanistic philosophy 130, 131
Meninges 119
Messenger molecules 28, 31
Microscope 97
Milky Way 104
Mind 116-133
Minimum required structures for life 36
Minos 8
Missing links 62, 107-115
Mitosis 29
Mitochondria 28, *28*

Molecular biology 79, 88
Molecular evolution 79
Molecules 30, 31, 36, 68-78, *100*, 101, 102
Mollusks 61, 62, *64*
Monkey at typewriter 77
Monod and Jacob 90
Monotype 67
Morpholysis 49, 51, *52, 53,* 56
Moth 83, *95*
Murres 13
Muscles, birds' 9, 10
Mutations 109

Natural selection 54, 55, 78, 81-85, 87, 94, *94, 95*
Naturalism 131
Nerve cells, 10 billion in brain 117
Nerves 119-127, *124*
Neuroglial cells 121
Neurons 119-127
Neurosciences 127
Neurospora 82
Newell, Dr. Norman D., quoted 61, 63, 112
Newton, Sir Isaac 48
Newton's theory of gravitation 132
Nicholas of Cusa 40
Nose, organ of smell 123
Nucleolus *30,* 31
Nucleotides 71, 74-79
Nucleus 29, 30, *30*

One-celled animals 31-37
Organic molecules *100*
Origin of Species, Darwin's 61, 63, 64
Oscillatoria spicullina 36
Owl *18, 19*
Oxygen produced by photosynthesis 45

Paleontology 112, 115
Paramecium *32, 33,* 37
Parameters 102
Peripatus 60
Park and Biggins 45
Phacus 35
Phasmid *94*
Photons 41
Photosynthesis 38-47
    schematic representation of *103*
Phyla 108, 109
Pigments in Coleus leaf 41
Pinacea 108
Pine needle, cross section of 46
Pinus 108
Plasma membrane 26
Plato, on brain 118
Platt, Rutherford, quoted 26
Plover, golden 10
Polymerase 34
Polypeptides 68-79
Porifera 62
Precambrian fossils 60, 61, *64*
Priestly, Joseph 40
"Primordial" cell 26, 36, 37
Probability 66, 67-79, *74,* 77
Processes essential to life 36
Protein molecules 26, 68-78
Proteins 67-79, 82
Protoplasm 26
Protozoa 37
Puffins 13

Quanta 41-45
Quantasomes 45
Quill 12

Rabbits *86,* 87
Rachis 12, *12*
Radiant energy 101, 102, *102*

141

Radical new design essential 84
Random changes 78, 79, 84
Reductionism 127
Renaissance
Repressor 89, 90, *90, 91*
Reproduction 29, 30, 51
Ribonucleic acid (*see* RNA)
Ribosomes 28, 29
Rivularia *35*
RNA 28, 31, 34, 36, 71-78 73
Rocky Mountains 59, 65

Sea anemone *106*
Sea lilies *109*
Sea urchins 109
Sea worms 59-61
Sensory receptors in birds' skin 13, 14
Serine molecule *69*
Sexual reproduction 29, 30
Shakespeare, quoted 118
Shearwaters 11, 15
Shrikes *95*
Sierra maple *43*
Sight, keen, of birds 11
Signals, electrochemical 123
Silver Lake *46, 47*
Simpson, Dr. George G., quoted 62, 63, 64, 112
Size, optimum 54, 55, 84
Skeletons, birds' 10
Slotting of wings *14, 16, 18*
Soaring flight 15, 16
Solar energy 38-45, *38, 39,* 102
Solomon, King 19
Specialization of cells 31
Species *85,* 107, 108, *108, 110, 111*
Spectroscope 104
Spectrum *102,* 102-104
Sperm 30
Spinal cord 119, 121

Spirostomum *37*
Sponges 61
Starch in leaf cells 41
Starch-splitting enzymes 68
Starfish *106,* 109
Stentor *32, 37*
Stroma 44
Structures, minimum, required for life 36
Sugar produced in leaf cells 41
Sun 38, *38,* 104
Survival value 82, 84
Swallows 22
Swan 11

Telescope 99
Temperature, birds' high body 10
Thalamus 121
Theistic evolutionist 79
Thermal currents 16
Thermodynamics, second law of 49
Thymine 71
"Toboggan" on air currents 15, *15,* 16
"Trees of life" 107, *110, 111, 114*
Trilobites *58,* 59, 60, *62, 63,* 64

Underwing moth, red *95*
Universe 48, 49
    energy of 52
Uracil 71

Variation 88
Visible spectrum *102*
Von Braun, Wernher 6, 7
Von Helmont 40
Vorticella *37*

Walcott, Charles 59
Water molecule in photosynthesis 43-45

Watson and Crick 30
Wavelengths of radiant energy 101, *102*
Wing-beat rate 19
Wing slot, birds' 13
Wings, birds' 10-19, *12, 14*
Wingspan of man-o'-war bird 10

Wonderful World of Life, The
    Julian Huxley's 107
Worm burrows, Precambrian 60, *64*
Worms, fossil 59-61
    segmented 59, 60
Yucca flower and moth 83